Glimpses of
the Civil War
in the Lower
Shenandoah Valley
1861-1862

Susan Crites

Published by
Butternut Publications
P.O. Box 1851
Martinsburg, West Virginia 25401

First Printing May 1996

Manufactured in the United States of America

DEDICATION

This book is dedicated to the people of Berkeley, Jefferson and Morgan counties whose lives were forever changed by the great War Between The States.

They lived valiantly, sacrificed courageously and endured more hardship for a longer period of time than any other Americans of their era.

Their true story must never be forgotten!

ACKNOWLEDGMENTS

Compiling an accurate history of the Civil War in the Lower Shenandoah Valley has been a research and writing challenge of a lifetime. During that long journey, innumerable people provided me with information, tutelage, advice and support. I am indebted to them all!

I am grateful to my parents who taught me that Civil War history is not a dry recitation of irrelevant events in a time long past. From them, I learned that Civil War history is the fascinating story of real people who lived in extraordinary times. My childhood family trips to Civil War battlefields, the Smithsonian Institution, the National Archives and other significant repositories of 19th century information made an indelible impression and created a life-long yearning to know more about the subject.

I am deeply indebted to the meticulous team of technical experts who have helped me, during the seemingly endless months, to bring this work to fruition. They are my gifted and discerning editor, Louise Kosco, my steadfast book designer and typesetter, Lesa Selders, and my tireless research associates, Esther Watson and Jeff Fink.

I would like to thank the descendants of those who lived in Berkeley, Jefferson and Morgan counties during the Civil War for their dedication to this project and for their abundant help.

I would also like to thank those who are the conservators of the documents that record the events of the time. Without them, this remarkable story would surely have been lost!

Finally, I would like to thank Thomas Ayrd, owner and publisher of the *Buyer's Guide*, Martinsburg, West Virginia. He gave me the opportunity to tell this remarkable story to thousands of readers!

INTRODUCTION

All too often, histories of the Civil War in the Shenandoah Valley tell us that when a Union army used the Potomac River crossings to invade the south, that army "went to Winchester, Virginia."

For someone who is not familiar with the geography of the region, it would be reasonable to assume from histories of this sort that Winchester is immediately adjacent to the Potomac River. It is not! In fact, it is sufficiently distant from the Potomac River crossings that the Union army did not approach Winchester until the spring of 1862!

During the Civil War, the northern border of the South was the Potomac River. When invading armies crossed the Potomac into Virginia they marched into Berkeley, Jefferson and Morgan counties. There they were met and their invasion was contested by the Virginia militia and by the Confederate army.

When Confederate General Johnston withdrew his army from its indefensible position at Harpers Ferry in the summer of 1861, they moved through Jefferson County to Bunker Hill in Berkeley County. General Lee's withdrawal from the battlefield at Antietam in the fall of 1862 took his army to safety in Shepherdstown in Jefferson County. Lee's perilous withdrawal from Gettysburg in the summer of 1863 ended when his army crossed the raging and swollen Potomac River into Berkeley County. J.E.B. Stuart's famous ride around the Union army began in Darkesville in Berkeley County.

Fighting in the Shenandoah Valley clearly did not begin and end in Winchester, Virginia. To fully understand the Civil War in the Shenandoah Valley, one must know about the consequential events that took place in the Lower Shenandoah Valley.

This book introduces the remarkable people of Berkeley, Jefferson and Morgan counties who lived there during the Civil War. In 1861, while most of the country, North and South, simply talked about the war, these courageous people endured the terror of skirmishing around their homes, the indignity of arrest and occupation by enemy troops and the heart-stopping anxiety that is an ever present reality for those who lived in a highly coveted part of the Shenandoah Valley. Their extraordinary story has almost been forgotten!

In this and three forthcoming volumes, I will share glimpses of the people and events that took place in the lower Shenandoah Valley during each campaign year of the war. This history is fresh, largely unknown and helps to complete the full and historically accurate picture of the Civil War in the Shenandoah Valley.

CONTENTS

WHERE IS THE LOWER SHENANDOAH VALLEY?

If you look at a topographical map, you will see that one end of the Shenandoah Valley has a higher elevation than the other. The northern end of the Valley, which is near the Potomac River, has the lower elevation. The southern end of the valley has the higher elevation.

It is easy to understand how early settlers, who traveled on foot, began a tradition in the Shenandoah Valley of saying that they were traveling "up the Valley" because they were literally climbing to a higher elevation. Conversely, if they said they were "going down the Valley," they meant they were descending from the higher elevation to the lower elevation.

As a consequence, the southern part of the Shenandoah Valley is known as the Upper Shenandoah Valley and the northern part of the Shenandoah Valley is known as the "Lower Shenandoah Valley."

Three of the lower Shenandoah Valley counties are Berkeley, Jefferson and Morgan counties. The northern border of these counties is defined by the Potomac River. During the Civil War, when Union armies invaded the South from Maryland, they first stepped foot in enemy territory in Berkeley, Jefferson or Morgan counties.

To further complicate understanding the location of this area, one must recall that these counties were Virginia counties until 1863. In that year, Abraham Lincoln signed a Presidential Proclamation designating portions of western Virginia as the 35th state in the Union to be known as West Virginia. Berkeley, Jefferson and Morgan were generously given to the new state. The people who lived there objected and preferred to remain a part of Virginia. The matter was settled several years later in the United States Supreme Court with the counties becoming a permanent part of West Virginia.

If one looks at a map of the 35th state, the three counties look to some like the handle of a pan. Over time, Berkeley, Jefferson and Morgan counties came to be known colloquially as the Eastern Panhandle of West Virginia.

The terms Lower Shenandoah Valley and Eastern Panhandle are used interchangeably. Those who prefer to emphasize their Virginia heritage use the Lower Shenandoah Valley to describe Berkeley, Jefferson and Morgan counties. Those who chose to emphasize their support for the creation of a new state of West Virginia by Unionist forces use the Eastern Panhandle of West Virginia to describe the same geographic area.

THE WEEK THE EASTERN PANHANDLE WENT TO WAR

During the first months of 1861, the conservative people of the Eastern Panhandle gradually gave up the notion that differences between the northern and southern states could be settled by the United States Congress and that the nation could be preserved. As states in the deep South seceded, a feeling of crisis developed. Many Panhandle residents, like Alfred M. Barbour of Jefferson County, moved from their positions of strong support for the Union to a reluctant acceptance of secession. Others, like Bethuel M. Kitchen of Berkeley County, denounced the ordinance as nothing less than treason. When President Abraham Lincoln proclaimed that an insurrection existed in the deep South and called for states to furnish 75,000 troops to crush the rebellion, Virginia's Governor John Letcher refused by saying, "The militia of Virginia will not be furnished to the powers at Washington for any such use or purpose as they have in view!" On April 17, the Virginia State Convention adopted an ordinance of secession by a vote of 88 to 55. Immediately following the vote, remarkable events began to take shape.

About 10:00 p.m. the next day, as a large force of Virginia militia was approaching from Halltown, the United States Armory in Harpers Ferry was abandoned and burned by its Union garrison. About an hour later, two brothers, Raleigh and William Colston, were walking home from drill with their militia company, the Hedgesville Blues. Both men noticed a bright light in the sky. William remarked that the light was probably the armory at Harpers Ferry. Raleigh disagreed and both went to bed. Shortly thereafter, they heard a call from under their bedroom window. A messenger had been sent from Martinsburg with orders from the commander of the militia to call out the Hedgesville Blues and report to Harpers Ferry as soon as possible. That night messengers with a call to war spread throughout the Panhandle.

April 19 was a cloudy day. At about 8:00 a.m., the Berkeley Border Guards and the Alburtis Artillery assembled in the town square at Martinsburg. Belle Boyd, who would soon become a Confederate spy, was on hand to watch the spectacle. "The enthusiasm of the enlistment was adequate to the occasion," she wrote in her memoirs. "Old men, with gray hairs and stooping forms, young boys, just able to shoulder a musket, strong and weak, rich and poor, rallied to our new standard, actuated by a stern sense of duty and eager for victory or death!" As martial music filled the town, and tearful families waved white handkerchiefs, Captain John Quincy Adams Nadenbouch gave the marching order. The men paraded to the train station, boarded the cars and went to war. The scene was repeated, time and again, throughout the area.

No one in the Eastern Panhandle could know, on that fateful day in April, that the Civil War would plunge them all into a hurricane of blood, battle, occupation and intrigue. Every life would be affected. Almost all would lose a loved one to an enemy bullet. Few citizens, anywhere in the country, would endure the unimaginable agony that would befall the people of the lower Shenandoah Valley. Yet, on that cloudy day, both Unionists and Confederates were filled with hope for their cause: a firm belief that the war would be short and they would be victorious.

COMMOTION AND CHAOS: THE FIRST WEEKS OF THE CIVIL WAR

The capture of the arsenal at Harpers Ferry in the spring of 1861 had an electric effect on the people of the lower Shenandoah Valley. The war was finally a reality. The Union flag had been lowered and the Virginia flag raised in its place. Everyone was filled with a restless expectation of what might come next. Most were caught up in a whirl of frantic activity.

At Harpers Ferry, men from the local infantry militia units, Berkeley Border Guards, (Martinsburg), Bott's Grey's (Charles Town), Floyd Guards (Harpers Ferry), Hamtramck Guards (Shepherdstown), Hedgesville Blues (Hedgesville), Jefferson Guards (Charles Town), Letcher Riflemen (Duffields) and the Morgan Continentals (Berkeley Springs) were mustered into 2nd Regiment, Virginia Volunteers of the Confederate Army. Not all men who reported during the first days mustered in. Some men were discharged as overage or infirm. Others escaped from their units and left the state. Union men streamed across the Potomac to join units being organized in Williamsport by Abraham Lincoln's law partner and former Panhandle resident, Ward Hill Lamon.

Local roads immediately became clogged with traffic.

Seven thousand men rushed to Harpers Ferry to enlist. Coaches and wagons, filled with friends and family, made frequent visits to the troops. Wagons accompanied by soldiers went near and far to purchase quartermaster supplies from local farms. People throughout the Panhandle traveled from home to home to talk about the war and bring the latest news.

The Potomac River became the border between North and South. From Harpers Ferry to McCoy's Ferry and Fort Frederick, it was heavily patrolled. Troops on both sides stood guard, reported activities on the opposite banks, and took potshots at one another. Ferryboats, row boats and canoes carried people from one side to the other. Some were escaping to their new country and others were spies.

Throughout the Panhandle, women were forming the first Sewing Societies. These societies would produce clothing, tents and all manner of equipment for their soldiers. Men who were not serving in the army patrolled the town streets. A local writer observed, "along the Border every man seemed to suppose he had the right to constitute himself a special constable, to arrest and question every other man he met with whose business he was not acquainted." Union supporters were harassed and arrested. Union-owned businesses were closed. Some families with men in service immediately became destitute and others living close to the

Potomac River, like the Colston family of Hedgesville, became the first refugees of the war when they went South to find safety.

Within days of the capture of Harpers Ferry, the quiet country lives of the people of the Eastern Panhandle began to unravel. Within weeks, activity at home, in the camps and in the countryside would reach a fever pitch.

BLOCKADE THE POTOMAC!
STARVE THE PEOPLE!

On April 16, 1861, President Abraham Lincoln, instituting economic warfare against the armies and civilians of the South, forbade trade of any kind with seceded states. In May, he proclaimed a blockade and sealed off "all Virginia east of the Alleghenies" as well as the Potomac River. From that time until the end of the war, this proclamation would cause more suffering among the people of the lower Shenandoah Valley than any other aspect of the war.

Before the war, the people of Berkeley , Jefferson, and Morgan counties were distinctly southern in their social, cultural, and political customs. They were Virginians, the proud, aristocratic descendants of the oldest families and noble leaders of the country. In addtion, the Baltimore and Ohio Railroad, a system of superb roads and stage coach lines provided easy, affordable access to Northern east coast cities, of which they readily took advantage. Many traveled often and became accustomed to buying a wide range of goods manufactured throughout the world. They read newspapers from Baltimore and New York, bought books from publishing houses in Boston and London, and most popular food in the area was oysters harvested from the nearby Chesapeake Bay. When the border was sealed, the shock, like a lightning bolt, of being cut off from anything produced in the North was painful for nearly everyone.

On May 27, 1861, United States Postmaster Montgomery Blair terminated postal service in the South "til the same can be safely restored. "All business that had been conducted by mail ground to a stop. Business with firms as close as Hagerstown and Hancock could not be conducted. Access to funds held in banks in the North was impossible and checks, drawn on banks North and South, became worthless in the absence of regular mail service. Within weeks of the seizure of the Armory at Harpers Ferry, the people of the border counties of Berkeley, Jefferson and Morgan were faced with the awful reality that they could only purchase items of local manufacture and that they had very little money available to them for that purpose.

Shortages, substitutions and doing without became a way of life. Within a few weeks, medicine, sugar, coffee, tea, salt, cloth, shoes, sewing needles, toys, gloves, hats, window glass, tools, farm implements, coal, the much beloved oysters, and more disappeared from store shelves and pantries. For the remainder of the war, the people would expend enormous amounts of energy providing for the basics of life: food to keep their families alive, clothing to protect them from the elements, a source of heat to prevent discomfort and illness during bitter winter weather and most importantly, salt, without which life cannot be sustained.

As President Lincoln had hoped, economic warfare against the armies and people of the South was an instant success. The suffering and hardships began immediately. The predictable war-time vermin of civilization materialized in the form of dangerous smugglers, greedy profiteers, and gloating hoarders. Just as the people of the lower Shenandoah Valley began to grasp the possibility that the war, the cannon balls and the bullets might kill them, they faced a second and far more deadly peril: a blockade of the Potomac.

Harper's Ferry in 1861

HARPERS FERRY AND BOLIVAR: THE TOWNS THAT DIED

In 1747 Robert Harper began to operate a ferry near the confluence of the Shenandoah and Potomac Rivers. A picturesque town named after Harper nestled at the base of the Blue Ridge Mountains, which rose breathtakingly from the river floor. When the charming town was incorporated in 1763, no one who lived in the vigorous, burgeoning community could have guessed that Harpers Ferry and Bolivar would be dead in less than one hundred years.

In the late 1790's, as an arsenal and armory were being established at Harpers Ferry, the town began to grow. Craftsmen, artisans and laborers moved to the town and many became property owners. For decades, the town's economic life centered around the United States armory which made many of the rifles used in the War of 1812 and the famous 1841 Model "Mississippi Rifle."

On April 18, 1861, in the first action of the Civil War on Virginia soil, the commander of the small Federal garrison stationed at Harpers Ferry learned that Virginia militia were advancing on the town. He set fire to the large armory and arsenal establishment that occupied the Potomac side of the town and led his troops across the railed bridge to safety in Maryland. Within minutes, Turner Ashby's cavalry thundered toward the lower part of the town. Citizens milled near the confluence of the rivers and the two railroads. All businesses, except saloons, had been closed that day as the people waited for something to happen. When the Virginia cavalry entered the town, some of the people set about plundering the Federal facility. Others formed groups to help fight the fires. Women cursed both Union and Virginia soldiers while men argued, wondering about the fate of their jobs and families.

For two months, the Confederate army occupied the towns. Enormous numbers of men from all over the South and men from the North who felt a kinship with the southern cause descended on Harpers Ferry. By the middle of May, fifteen thousand men had converged on Harpers Ferry and Bolivar. A North Carolina soldier named N.H. Dawson watched civilian life in the towns as the army buried them under the weight of men and materiel. He wrote to his fiancé that "most of the respectable families had fled from the place" and that "a lady was seldom to be seen on the streets."

For the remainder of the war, armies and their soldiers took public buildings, churches, private homes, even ruins of buildings, and used them to suit their purposes. Nothing was sacred. Churches were used as stables. The insatiable need for wood stripped the entire mountain side of the upper town and Bolivar of trees, leaving it bare, eroded and hideous. The area was continuously in motion as troops, animals, supplies, deserters, informers and opportunists passed through the towns. Hogs, dogs and buzzards fed on the developing squalor.

The Harpers Ferry/Bolivar area served many purposes for both armies. It was a vast camp, a jumping off place for invading armies, a collection of filthy, lice-infested prison pens, a supply dump and a frequent battle site. Its new population was made up of transients, many of them the worst and most dangerous of people. Officer's wives, treasury agents, sutlers, nurses, smugglers, refugees, escaped slaves, outlaws and hooligans formed a boiling mass of humanity who shared little in common except indifference to the towns.

By war's end, the area had become a place of dirty desolation that visitors repeatedly described as a ruin, filled with rubbish, nastiness and stench. Whatever price others in the country might pay because of the civil war, the people of Harpers Ferry and Bolivar had given everything. Their towns had died.

BATTLING FOR BOATS:
THE FIRST SKIRMISH

In mid-May 1861, Colonel Thomas J. Jackson, commanding Virginia's troops at Harpers Ferry, was concerned about Berkeley County. In a letter to Robert E. Lee he said, " I regret to say that in Berkeley [County] things are growing worse, and that threats from Union men are calculated to curb the expression of Southern feeling. While I have been unwilling to diminish the force here, for the purpose of checking disloyalty there, I have ordered the regiment from Jefferson [County] opposite to Williamsport."

The regiment Jackson ordered to Berkeley County was the Second Regiment of Virginia Volunteers. It was composed of ten companies and commanded by the one-eyed V.M. I. graduate, Colonel James Walkinson Allen of Jefferson County. Men from all three Eastern Panhandle counties served in this regiment.

On May 17, they established Camp Allen on the Virginia shore across the river from Williamsport and spread along the Potomac River to the east and west. On the Maryland side, the river was guarded by refugees from the Eastern Panhandle who had joined the First Virginia Volunteers (USA) and by the local Home Guards.

Within shouting distance, the two forces continually harassed one another. The harassment was more mischief-making than war-like. At McCoy's Ferry, Southern troops patrolling there decided to steal several small boats they could see resting on the Maryland shore. In the dark of night they embarked on their adventure and rowed across the Potomac. They were in the act of stealing the boats when the Clear Spring Home Guard heard their noise and rushed at them from their quarters in a local farmer's home. They sent a hail of fire at the Virginians and leapt for cover when the shots were returned. The Virginians in the boats, realizing that they were easy targets, jumped out of the boats into the river and disappeared. Both sides claimed to have injured the enemy in this, the first skirmish of the war along the Potomac. The boats were recovered and returned to their owner.

As the weeks passed, the opposing forces stationed along the Potomac skirmished often over boats and ferries. Civilians living near the river were the first in the Eastern Panhandle to learn that the war would take place in and around their homes, that their loved ones and property were at terrible risk. They learned to dread and fear the sound of gunfire. As injuries from the mild skirmishing mounted, the soldiers on both sides began to realize that this great, romantic adventure could become a killing war.

PANHANDLE UNIONISTS: CUT OFF, LONELY AND AFRAID

"I am a Virginian, every drop of blood that flows in my veins is Virginian, but my being Virginian don't make me a Secessionist—it, on the contrary, makes me a Unionist, for I think Va.'s good is in holding to the Union, to the Constitution and to the Laws."
Sallie Pendleton Van Rensselaer, Berkeley Springs

Early in the Civil War the lower Shenandoah Valley was a Confederate stronghold. Unionists, those who held for the Union and who voted against the secession of Virginia, were at terrible risk. Union officer and Panhandle resident David Strother described them by saying that those who were formerly conspicuous for their "free, frank and kindly air, warm with jovial living and insouciance" now carried "the haggard impress of terror, anxiety and suspicion." They spoke in an undertone while "anxiously scanning windows and doors."

The Pendleton family, the Strothers, the Campbells, Dr. Richard McSherry, David H. Conrad, John S. Bowers, Bethuel Kitchen, Christian Shaeffer, Rev. Charles W. Andrews, Joseph Welshans, and others were considered traitors by Confederates. Every Unionist was a well-known object of fanatical hatred by many. They

21

were arrested frequently, sometimes daily. They were ridiculed by neighbors, robbed or terrorized by soldiers and forced to endure humiliating loyalty hearings. Confederate shopkeepers and farmers refused to sell them goods of any kind. Communication with family and friends in the North was cut off. They avoided social contact and lived in a continual state of anxiety.

Harassing Unionists was a favored pastime of Confederate troops. Phillip Pendleton, the aging patriarch of the prominent Pendleton family and the wealthiest man in Berkeley County, was standing in front of his home in Martinsburg when a company of Confederate cavalrymen rode by. Recognizing the influential Unionist, they gave three loud cheers for Confederate President Jefferson Davis and three awful groans for Union President, Abraham Lincoln.

Unionists complained bitterly that their property was at the mercy of "the whim or greed" of Confederate troops and their government. David Strother's home and that of his father in Berkeley Springs were ransacked by Confederate troops. They carried off bedding, furniture, silverware, picture frames, and even a little girl's doll house furniture. Strother believed that the property was destroyed out of "mere spite and malignity."

Within months, the tide of battle would turn and the

Union army would occupy the lower Shenadoah Valley. All that the Unionists had endured during the Confederate occupation would be visited upon the Confederate loyalists during the Union occupation. Each time the area changed hands, the treatment of enemy loyalists became more harsh. Not a man, woman or child who lived in the area during the war would escape the awful wrath of the enemy, the armies and their own neighbors.

THE FIRST BATTLE AT
FALLING WATERS

Every morning for days, the people of Bedington, Hainesville, Falling Waters and parts of Martinsburg were awakened an hour before dawn by the roar of cannon. For two long hours the cannon boomed. Babies cried, animals shied in their pens or ran madly about the fields, farm wives couldn't bake for fear that the bread would fall, farmers weren't able to plow with terrified horses, nearby windows shattered, houses shook and people grew edgy. The canonniers of Col. Thomas Jackson's command were learning their trade and the people of Berkeley County were paying the price.

Jackson and his troops were camped in an oak forest four miles north of Martinsburg, just below the south tributary of Hokes Run, on the west side of the Williamsport Pike. In late June 1861, rumors were rampant that an invasion across the Potomac from Williamsport into Berkeley County by Union General Robert Patterson's troops was imminent. Jackson had been sent to keep an eye on Patterson. Jackson kept his cavalry busy patrolling along the Potomac and the rest of his men engaged in learning to be soldiers.

On the morning of July 2, 1861, a cavalryman thundered into camp with the news that advance troops of

Patterson's army were invading. Immediately the camp burst into activity. Col. Kenton Harpers 5th Regiment and Rev. Pendleton's Rockbridge Artillery assembled for a northward scout.

Jackson led his column down the Williamsport Pike to a rise about five miles south of the Potomac. At 7:30 a.m., the Virginians saw Union troops, hundreds of them, with flags flying and drums beating, in line of battle just a half mile down the road. The untrained Valley troops broke from their ranks, climbing on rocks, fences and into trees for a better look at the incredible sight. Even the untrained man could see that the 350 Confederates were badly outnumbered. In an instant, the Federal troops fired on the Confederates who leapt and dodged for cover.

Jackson quickly positioned his men at the edge of a nearby woods facing an open field and sent sharpshooters to occupy William Porterfield's house and barn. Pendleton wheeled his six-pound cannon to a position covering the road. Federal troops advanced and were repulsed. Firing was heavy and erratic for an hour. As Jackson watched the battle unfold, he sat astride his horse under an oak tree on the side of the pike. When a bullet whizzed overhead and clipped off a branch of the tree, he said, "They have gotten our range. I suppose we had better retire." The Confederates im-

mediately started a fire and retreat, fire and retreat, retrograde movement.

When the Confederates had withdrawn several hundred yards, the Union troops swarmed forward. Union
cavalry charged down the pike almost into the mouth
of Sandy Pendleton's cannon. He ordered his
cannoniers to fire aiming for the horse's knees. Their
solid shot cleared the pike of Union cavalry. Immediately, the two Union cannon batteries began to roar,
firing thirty-five times at the withdrawing Confederates. Jackson ordered his men to fall back on the 2nd
and 4th Regiments that had dashed forward to assist
and to guard the three guns left behind as reserve. When
his men were safely behind the powerful guns, Jackson seemed willing to continue the fight. But Patterson
had enough and by 10:30 a.m. the First Battle at Falling Waters was over.

As the smoke cleared, the Confederates marched
through Martinsburg taking forty Union prisoners with
them. William Porterfield's house and barn were
riddled with bullets and in flames. The countryside
was littered with the debris of battle and the bodies of
twenty men who had died that morning. As the people
nearby warily emerged from their homes, they saw what
few civilians in the lower Shenandoah Valley had ever
seen, the grisly, frightening specter of a killing war.

As the sun rose higher and hotter, they thought about the blue uniformed troops beginning to swarm around them. They were more afraid than they had ever been in their lives.

THE VENGENCE OF
NIMROD D. KENEASTER

In the early summer of 1861 the people of the Eastern Panhandle lived lives full of passion. Secessionists and Unionists alike believed in their cause with vehemence. And the presence of a burgeoning Confederate Army made life difficult for outspoken Unionists. One such man was Nimrod D. Keneaster.

Keneaster was a merchant who lived and operated a general store one-half mile from Martinsburg on the Williamport Pike. He and his wife Mary Ann lived in what was once the old homestead of local banker Daniel Burkhart. Life had not been kind to the couple. Three little girls had been born to them during their marriage. In 1845, 1852 and 1857 each child died at the age of eleven. N.D. Keneaster was known to be a bitter and angry man.

On June 12, 1861, fate gave Keneaster an outlet for his inner rage. On that day he rented a safe from a Mr. Locke. He arranged the rental through Locke's attorney, John Weller. After the papers were signed, Keneaster removed the safe from Locke's home and installed it in the back of his general store

Within days of the rental, as Unionists were being arrested in Martinsburg, Keneaster joined others in a wild flight for safety across the Potomac border and into Maryland. Keneaster took only his wife and a few belongings. That same day, a Confederate Colonel named Oliver Funsten came looking for Keneaster and found him gone. He immediately "impressed" or impounded all of Keneaster's property for use by the Confederacy. Word reached Mr. Locke's attorney that everything at Keneaster's place was being carried off and he went there to explain that the safe belonged to Locke not Keneaster. Eventually, he was able to reclaim the safe. It was empty but, he had been told that the safe had contained two or three hundred dollars in Confederate money. That money had been confiscated by Colonel Funsten and deposited at Martinsburg in the Bank of Berkeley.

When the Union army invaded Berkeley County in July 1861, Keneaster returned to the county. Finding his safe gone, he went to the Union authorities and asked for the arrest of the lawyer, John Weller. Weller was arrested and taken before J. H. Lockwood, the Provost Marshall. At that time, Keneaster wanted his money back and he insisted that Weller repay. He claimed there had been eight or nine hundred dollars in the safe. Since the Provost Marshall knew that Keneaster was "a man who was determined to make money without regard to the character or the means of the effort," he released Weller.

Martinsburg changed hands again. When the Union

army returned, Keneaster had Weller arrested again. Keneaster had become friendly with the new Provost Marshall, John Weyland and invited Weyland to board at his home. Together they determined to force the lawyer to pay.

The Provost Marshall and Keneaster kept Weller in jail for several days. They threatened to take everything he owned if Weller did not repay the money. Weller refused, insisting he had not taken the money. Finally, Weyland and Keneaster made their last offer. To avoid being shipped north to prison, Weller was allowed to post a bond in the amount of $950.00, by putting up an expensive carriage and four horses as security for the bond, which would be held by Keneaster until the matter could be settled in a civil court at the end of the war. When Weller was finally released, he did not trust the word of the vindictive Keneaster and left the state that day. Later, he would learn that the Provost Marshall sent troops to his house an hour after his release to arrest him yet again.

Following the war, Keneaster would sue Weller nine separate times and lose each time. He was finally ordered to return the security for the $950.00 bond to John Weller. In a notarized statement, he said he could not return the security since it had been stolen by Confederate troops. Until the day he died, Keneaster kept Weller's carriage in his barn.

The tales of bitter feelings over the Civil War between neighbors in the Eastern Panhandle are true. Some were bitter to have lost loved ones in battle. Others were bitter to have suffered indignity and abuse at the hands of the enemy. More than a few were like the lawyer John Weller, bitter to have been victimized by a raging man who could use the enormous power of army to fight his private battles.

BELLE BOYD:
REBEL PATRIOT AND SPY

*"One of the most active and most reliable of
the many secret agents of the Confederacy."*
                              -Douglas Southall Freeman

On July 4, 1961, Union troops celebrated Independence Day in Martinsburg. A noisy celebration was held while Pennsylvania troops commanded by General Robert Patterson spread through the town.

A local distillery, owned by Confederate Colonel John Quincy Adams Nadenbousch, was ransacked and its potent product was eagerly consumed by the celebrating soldiers. Soon, they broke into the home of Martinsburg merchant, Benjamin Reed Boyd. Boyd was serving with Company D of the Second Virginia Infantry, CSA, and he was with those troops who were laying in line-of-battle on the outskirts of the city, unable to protect his family. The soldiers rampaged through Reed's home as his horrified wife and family watched helplessly. They broke furniture, smashed family heirlooms and threatened the women with all manner of violence.

The troops were in the Boyd house to find and capture a Confederate flag said, by a local Unionist informer, to be hanging in one of the bedrooms. Failing to find the flag, the men proposed to raise a Union flag over the Rebel household. As Mrs. Boyd refused, she stood by her seventeen year old daughter, Belle, and said, "Men, every member of my household will die before that flag shall be raised over us."

The soldiers erupted in anger at the provocative statement and damned the arrogant Rebel women. Belle, furious over the entire incident and outraged at the treatment of her mother, pulled a pistol from the folds of her skirt, shot and killed one of the men. While the Union Provost Marshall did not press charges against Belle because of the damage to their home and drunken condition of the soldiers, the incident transformed her into a fiery enemy.

Belle Boyd immediately began to collect information about Union troop strength, disposition and plans by charming information from Union officers. She always got the information swiftly to nearby Confederate troops. As a cunning and resourceful spy she gave great service to Confederate leaders. Among them were J.E.B. Stuart during the Union invasion of the lower Shenandoah Valley in 1861 and to Stonewall Jackson during his Shenandoah Valley campaign. She was twice arrested on orders from the War Department in Washington, DC and imprisoned for her activities. She escaped to England in 1863 because she was, by that time, subject to the death penalty for treason.

While there were innumerable spies for both sides who plied their secret trade in the lower Shenandoah Valley during the Civil War, Belle Boyd is said to have been the most romantic and cunning of them all.

FIRST AMONG CONFEDERATES: THE REMARKABLE FAULKNER FAMILY

When Mary, the youngest child of Brigadier General Elisha Boyd, married Charles James Faulkner in September of 1833, she could not have known that their lives were to be touched by destiny, that they would become one of the most famous families in the Confederacy. Her father was a well known lawyer and highly respected Virginian. He had been a hero in the 1812 war with Great Britain, served in the Virginia House of Delegates and the Virginia Senate, represented Berkeley County at the 1830 Constitutional Convention, and served as Attorney General of Virginia. Her father-in-law, Major James Faulkner, was a well known Martinsburg merchant and hero of the War of 1812 who was honored by the Virginia House of Delegates with a resolution of thanks. The marriage of Mary and Charles was the most important social event of the year in the lower Shenandoah Valley.

In 1841, Mary Boyd Faulkner inherited her father's magnificent mansion in Martinsburg known as Boydville. In that idyllic setting, they raised a family while Charles practiced law and became increasingly active in the political area as a leader in the anti-slavery movement. Thirty years before the outbreak of the civil war, in the famous debate on slavery in the Virginia Legislature, he said, "You must adopt some plan of emancipation, or worse will follow!" His courageous advocacy for emancipation brought him nationwide attention and the admiration of many of the most important men of the time. He was subsequently elected to the Congress of the United States.

President Buchanan appointed Charles James Faulkner Ambassador to France and the court of Napoleon Bonaparte in 1859. While Mary remained at Boydville with the younger children, Charles served with admirable distinction until the outbreak of the civil war, when President Abraham Lincoln recalled him.

Upon his arrival in the United States from France, Charles went to Washington to pay his respects to President Lincoln and Secretary of War Seward and to settle his affairs with the Department of State. Just as he completed this business, he was arrested and thrown into prison as a hostage for James McGraw, a Pennsylvania state official who had been captured at the battle of Manassas. Weeks later, he discovered that McGraw had been released. When he asked why he was still being held, he was told that he was no longer a hostage but was now a prisoner of war. He had refused to take the Oath of Allegiance to the United States. President Lincoln disapproved of Faulkner's arrest but failed to intercede on the Ambassador's behalf. The nation's newspapers howled in outrage that so distinguished a person should be held prisoner on such flimsy charges. The diplomatic community was appalled. Throughout his term of office, Lincoln would be haunted by the arrest of Faulkner and the seeds of distrust of his administration it had sewn in the minds of diplomats throughout the world.

After six months of uncomfortable and humiliating captivity, a reluctant Jefferson Davis intervened and released a U.S. Senator, also captured at Manassas, in return for Faulkner. Davis and Faulkner stood on opposite sides of the emancipation issue and did not like one another. Some said that Davis thought it was amusingly ironic that Faulkner should be jailed by abolitionist Northerners. Only the weight of public opinion in the South forced Davis to act.

When Faulkner returned to Martinsburg and his family, he was welcomed by the entire community. A dinner was given in his honor where he was congratulated for his distinguished service as Ambassador and his courage as a Virginian. At that dinner, he spoke with Alexander Boteler of Jefferson County. Boteler encouraged Faulkner to join the Confederate army and offered to introduce him to General "Stonewall" Jackson. Soon, Faulkner would leave Mary, his young children and Boydville to become Chief Of Staff for the great General Jackson.

AFTER MANASSAS:
A DARK AND STIRRING NIGHT

On a sultry afternoon in late July 1861, a messenger burst into a meeting of the Martinsburg City Council bearing news of a great Confederate victory in battle near the Manassas Railroad Junction and a creek called Bull Run. Wild cheering erupted but was soon silenced by the remainder of the news. A great number of men from the Eastern Panhandle had been slaughtered in the battle. Many more had been grievously wounded.

Soon word spread throughout the lower Shenandoah Valley counties of the battle on July 21st. It was said that the men and boys of the 2d Virginia Infantry had distinguished themselves, standing courageously, firmly, shoulder to shoulder, with Thomas Jonathan Jackson on Henry House Hill. The survivors of the great battle would serve as members of the legendary Stonewall Brigade but the price had been enormous!

The spring wagons, covered with oak boughs and bearing the dead, reached Martinsburg on the night on July 23rd. People gathered along the Winchester Pike and at the Norbourne Cemetary near Boydville to beg for news of their friends and loved ones from the grim-faced drivers. Wherever the wagons arrived in the Panhandle that night, the scene was the same: shock, horror, tears and grief. It would be remembered as one of the saddest nights of the war. "By the struggling moonbeam's misty light, our lanterns dimly burning," said one mourner, "we buried the truest sons of Virginia."

The stunned young widow of Peyton Harrison watched in disbelief as her husband was lifted from the wagon in a flimsy box that had been hurriedly nailed together and filled with the bodies of Peyton and his two young cousins, Holmes and Tucker Conrad. Word spread throughout Martinsburg that the young men had died in each other's arms. Their father, the well-known lawyer and Unionist, Robert Conrad, couldn't believe that his sons had run off to war and that the first news he had received about them was of their deaths. As she watched the three bodies being lowered into the same tomb, the widow Harrison felt little consolation when she was told that her own brother, Robert Waterman Hunter, had chased and killed the Union Zouave who had shot her husband.

By morning the enormity of the tragedy was well known. More than thirty Confederate soldiers from Berkeley County alone had been killed and wounded in a single day. Fathers, sons, and brothers of most leading families in the area were casualties. Everyone seemed to know someone who had been killed or wounded in the battle. While some families jumped into their wagons to journey to wounded loved ones in a hospital at Front Royal that had been set up to care for the wounded from Manassas, others families shuttered their windows to grieve in darkened parlors.

For days the towns were strangely silent. People spoke in whispers and the air almost seemed thick with the smell of freshly dug graves. The people of Berkeley, Jefferson and Morgan counties were no strangers to the sudden violence and capriciousness of war. In the three months since the secession of Virginia, they had learned to fear the daily intrusions, arrests, threats and occasional violence that had been their brief wartime experience, but nothing had prepared them for the atrocious killing and maiming that came from the battle at Manassas Junction. After that dark and stirring burial night , there was no one left in the Panhandle who believed that this war could be won without an agony and sacrifice unparalleled in the history of the people of Virginia.

THE LOWER SHENANDOAH VALLEY PAID DEARLY FOR VICTORY AT THE FIRST BATTLE OF MANASSAS, JULY 21, 1861.

At approximately 2:45 p.m. on Sunday, July 1861, Confederate Brigadier General Barnard Elliot Bee, attempting to rally his men for the final phase of the battle of Manassas, called out, "There stands Jackson like a stonewall. Let us determine to die here and we will conquer." Bee's rallying cry forever named the man, Thomas Johnathan "Stonewall" Jackson and his brigade, the Stonewall Brigade.

The following men from Berkeley, Jefferson and Morgan Counties stood with Jackson in that stonewall and are known causalities of the battle.

(WIA-Wounded In Action, WIA/DOW-Wounded In Action and Died of Wounds, KIA- Killed In Action)

Alburtis, Ephraim G.	WIA
Armstrong, John S.	WIA
Asquith, Archibald	WIA
Billings, Henry M.	WIA
Buchanan, Thomas S.	WIA
Butler, Francis G.	WIA/DOW
Colbert, Joseph W.	WIA

Conrad, Henry Tucker	KIA
Conrad, Holmes A.	KIA
Dandridge, Edmund	WIA
Dugan, John A	WIA
English, Robert M.	WIA
Faulkner, Elisha Boyd	WIA
Fryatt, John T.	KIA
Gall, George W.	WIA
Glenn, William Y.	WIA
Grubbs, Epaminondas	KIA
Harrison, Peyton R.	KIA
Hastings, Daniel B.	WIA
Hendricks, William	KIA
Hines, James E.W.	WIA/DOW
Hobson, William C.	WIA
Hunter, David	WIA
Hurst, Thomas N.	WIA/DOW
Isler, Charles H.	WIA
Kelly, George William	WIA
Kidd, Thomas	WIA
Lashorn, Jacob	WIA
Light, William H.	WIA
Manning, William Price	WIA
Manor, Charles	WIA
Manor, David	KIA
McArdle, Owen	KIA
McCleary, Charles F.M.	WIA
McGarey, William	WIA
McMullen, Lambert	WIA

Miller, George W.	WIA
Mitchell, Charles M.	KIA
Myers, George N.	WIA/DOW
Noland, Gilmore	WIA
Ogden, Randolph K.	WIA
Page, Richard	WIA/DOW
Powell, L.W.	WIA
Rowan, John W.	WIA
Seibert, A.	WIA
Seibert, W.	WIA
Simmons, Joseph	WIA
Smith, G.S.	WIA
Strayer, D.	WIA
Timberlake, Seth M.	WIA
Triplett, James W.	WIA
Trussell, James M.	WIA
Welch, John	WIA
Whitson, George	WIA
Young, William H.	KIA

IRON HORSES ON THE MARTINSBURG PIKE

In June 1861, Colonel Thomas Johnathan Jackson, commanding four regiments of Virginia Volunteers, six companies of cavalry and a field battery of artillery, made his headquarters four miles north of Martinsburg at a place they named Camp Stevens. His men were busy destroying the Baltimore and Ohio Railroad facilities in Jefferson, Berkeley and Morgan counties and patrolling the border of the Confederacy along the Potomac River.

Throughout the area tracks were torn up, railroad ties were burned, and bridges were destroyed. When the bridges were gone, railroad cars were run over the edge of the tracks and plunged down into massive heaps that blocked streams and roadways for many months. At the magnificent railroad facility in Martinsburg, company after company of men worked feverishly on its total destruction. All the valuable railroad equipment and tools were collected and sent by wagon train to Winchester. Telegraph lines and equipment were carefully dismantled and sent south. Everything else was put to the torch. The beautiful white, limestone Colonnade Bridge over Burke Street, a gift from the B & O Railroad to the people of Martinsburg, was blown up.

Under the withering glares of the now-unemployed

railroaders and their families, the Confederate troops set about destroying the locomotives, passenger and freight cars that were gathered on the tracks in the middle of the of the facility. With their whistles tied open, thirty-five locomotives were loaded with coal and torched. Martinsburg filled with smoke. For many nights, the town was brightly lit by the extensive fires, while locomotive whistles shrieked and no one slept.

At the height of the destructive frenzy, a contemplative engineer in Jackson's command, Col. Thomas S. Sharp approached his commanding officer with a remarkable idea. He suggested that the destruction of the cars and locomotives should be halted. Since the Confederacy was desperately short of rolling stock of every kind, he reasoned that the locomotives and cars should be saved and sent south. The obvious problem with Sharp's idea was that the railroad bridge over the Opequon Creek had already been completely destroyed. This prevented Jackson from sending the cars by rail to Harpers Ferry and then south. Sharp suggested that the solution was to haul the cars overland from Martinsburg to Winchester.

Jackson authorized Sharp's plan and a new flurry of activity erupted. The locomotives were dug out of the debris and stripped of every unnecessary part to decrease the drag weight. The blacksmiths in the army and living in the area were put to work fashioning wide metal tires that were mounted on the wheels of the cars. Crews of soldiers cut timber and strengthened bridges across streams on the pike from the southern end of Martinsburg into Winchester. Every horse in Berkeley County was requisitioned by the Confederate commander and farmers from the far flung corners of the county were ordered to assemble at the station.

Hundreds of citizens and soldiers stood in wide-eyed amazement as teams of four horses, with a rider for every team, were hitched to the locomotives. When thirty-two horses were hitched in a line, the order was given to move forward. Slowly, the ponderous "Iron Horse" inched up the steep hill toward Queen Street. As the remarkable procession made its way through Martinsburg onto the road to Winchester, everyone along its route stopped to gawk. It was the most extraordinary image anyone had ever seen!

From that hot summer day until mid-March when Union troops recaptured the town, the work of moving cars and locomotives to the south continued. More than thirty locomotives and three hundred freight and passenger cars made the trip overland. Advancing Federal cavalry troops forced Confederate engineers to abandon two locomotives just outside of Martinsburg. For the remainder of the war, whole armies would pass them and wonder how locomotives came to be sitting on a road that was intended for travelers on foot, in wagons and on horseback. While passing troops may have wondered about the strange locomotives, the people of Berkeley County did not. They were simply another example of the madness that was engulfing them and beginning to totally control their lives.

THE WRATH OF THE ELEPHANT

The most important question in the minds of young men who had just enlisted to fight in the Civil War was what it would be like when they "saw the elephant" for the first time. The elephant was a euphemism for battle, destruction, death, and dying.

As the vibrant colors of fall began to peak on the hills and mountains of the Eastern Panhandle in 1861, the civilian population knew that while some had seen the elephant, all had certainly felt it's wrath!

Around the supper tables in the quiet homes of the lower Shenandoah Valley, families reflected on the rapid changes the Civil War had brought to their lives. In the spring, they believed the war would be won in three months or less. Instead of victory, the war was dragging on. In a stunningly swift series of events, many of the men and boys had become a part of armies and had left the Valley, the railroad line had been destroyed, stage coach and mail service had been stopped, the Potomac was blockaded, the local newspapers were no longer produced, manufactured goods and the money to buy them was becoming scarce. The schools, banks, many of the churches, and government services had ceased to function. While they tried to go about their daily business as if nothing had changed, they could not. The things they had taken for granted were gone. Their world had collapsed.

In solemn voices, they discussed their unexpected personal losses. Two armies had occupied the area. Their destruction of private property had been shocking. Confederate Col. John Quincy Adams Nadenbousch's home had been ransacked. His distillery had been looted and burned. The entire stock of Unionist A.R. McQuilken's General Store had been carried away. Private homes from the Potomac River to Charlestown, Bunker Hill and Berkeley Springs had been entered, searched, ransacked and some had been burned. Everyone had suffered some loss of crops, merchandise, live stock, poultry, fence posts, and family heirlooms that had been taken by one army or the other. In one home in Berkeley Springs, soldiers had stolen a little girl's doll house and furniture. Women throughout the Panhandle mourned the senseless destruction in their homes, crockery taken from cabinets and smashed, bed linen's ripped apart, family portraits slashed, children's toys broken, family treasures hurled through windows or stolen and much more. No one felt safe in this new world.

Perhaps, the most painful recollection that fall was about people. They had seen neighbors going out of their way to inform on their neighbors. When the Confederate Army controlled the area, Unionists were arrested. When the Union armed was in control, Confederates were arrested. Everyone had been stopped and questioned by one army or the other. News from the army camps was worse than news about some people in the community. Many dear friends and neighbors were already crippled for life and dead. Some had died of disease in the camps. George Dugan's son James had been shot through the chest and lung accidentally while on guard at Harpers Ferry. A local newspaper editor had shot off his own thumb. The skirmishing along the Potomac and the battles at Falling Waters and Manassas had taken a terrible toll on the men from the Eastern Panhandle. Some still cried when they thought about the popular young Peyton Harrison being killed at Manassas on the day of Peyton Junior's first birthday.

In that fall of 1861, most people in the country, even in places as near as Winchester, had not experienced the terror of fighting in their own back yards or the humiliation and brutality of occupation by an enemy army. Those people still felt the exultation and thrill of a painless Civil War. The people of the Eastern Panhandle, on the other hand, had felt the snarling, life threatening wrath of the elephant. They prayed deeply that the war would end and that their lives could somehow be put back together again. Over those somber supper tables throughout the Eastern Panhandle, most knew that their prayers could not be answered.

A VERY DIFFERENT THANKSGIVING

Many people consider Thanksgiving Day, as celebrated in the United States, to be the nation's oldest celebration of gratitude, dating from 1621. School children learn that when the first harvest was completed by the Plymouth colonists, Massachusetts Governor William Bradford proclaimed a day of thanksgiving, prayer, and feasting on the wealth of the harvest.

When the Civil War erupted in the spring of 1861, Thanksgiving Day was not a national holiday. It was a northern holiday, celebrated largely in the states of New England and New York. Secular or non-religious festivals and feasts were known in the South. Harvest festivals and feasts were often held following the successful gathering of summer crops. Celebrations and prayers commemorating the final separation between great Britain and her American colonies were observed throughout the country, North and South.

During the Civil War, the people were called by the Presidents of both nations to set aside a day of prayer and thanksgiving. These special days had little in common with modern Thanksgiving. None were observed by the people of the Eastern Panhandle.

Following the Confederate victory at the battle of

Manassas, President Jefferson Davis urged the loyal people of the South to observe July 28, 1861, as a day of fasting and prayer for the success of all southern armies in defending their homes. Four months later, President Abraham Lincoln designated November 28 as a Northern day of thanks that loyal men were fighting for their country. In the Eastern Panhandle, diarists both Unionist and Confederate, do not mention that these holidays were observed. The telegraph lines were dismantled. Mail was not moving to the lower Shenandoah Valley from the South or North. Newspapers were completely unavailable. No one knew that the holidays had been proclaimed.

More than two years passed before a day of thanksgiving was again proclaimed. President Lincoln called for a suspension of business and a day of prayer on August 6, 1863, to celebrate his proclamation of emancipation. Two months later on October 3, Lincoln issued another proclamation of thanksgiving. In it he designated the last Thursday of November as a day for the observance of thanks for military victory and "in humble penitence for our national perverseness and disobedience." This proclamation established the traditional date for the celebration of a day of thanksgiving that continues today.

Days of thanksgiving during the Civil War were proclaimed for political reasons, to underscore victory and to promote a new public policy of freedom for enslaved blacks.

On that October day in 1863 when President Lincoln established the day that would become modern Thanksgiving, the people of the Eastern Panhandle were starving. The policy of the Lincoln administration was to allow disloyal persons to continue to starve. Well-known Unionist citizens were allowed to buy meager supplies from Permit Stores. The stores opened on thanksgiving day 1863. No one in the Eastern Panhandle was given a permit to buy food on that Thanksgiving Day.

Days of thanksgiving were not days of celebration for the citizens of the Eastern Panhandle during the Civil War. The people lived in battle zones and amid increasingly brutal armies of occupation. The cruel destruction of property, civilian deaths from disease and war, and the gradual deterioration of an entire people were realities unknown to most people in all states for most of the war. Elsewhere, there was time and passion for political celebrations of thanksgiving. In the Eastern Panhandle, there was only the daily attempt to survive.

A CONFEDERATE WOMAN
DECIDES TO SURVIVE

As Sarah Forrest Harrison sits down to a breakfast of hot bread, ham, salt beef and cheese on the morning of November 21, 1861, she realizes that her husband Peyton has been dead exactly four months. A Union bullet had killed him in a battle at the Manassas Railroad Junction. She also thinks about her five month old son, Randolph, who died of a disease just three weeks before his father was killed. While she is surrounded at the table by the exuberant voices of the seven children and young people in her household, she thinks somberly about how her world has been changed by the war.

It seems to her that Martinsburg itself looks shabby. Public buildings like the Court House and churches have been badly damaged by troops of both armies. The railroad facility and train tracks are destroyed. Businesses and homes are burned to the ground throughout town. Most homes have at least one window boarded or covered with canvas because there is no glass available for replacements. The streets are deeply rutted by the thousands of men, wagons, horses and artillery caissons that have battered them since the war began in April. When it rains, mud on the side streets becomes deep enough to trap and smother a small child. Along the roads leading from Martinsburg to Sheperdstown, Williamsport and Winchester, the rotting carcasses and bleached-white bones of dead horses and mules are plainly visible. The beauty of the Shenandoah Valley seems lost.

The people look haggard to Sarah. Fear for the safety of their families and anxiety about the welfare of their loved ones in the army has begun to etch deep lines in many faces. The armies have brought disease to the town and so many children and old people have died from contact with the armies. Some, who have loved ones fighting in both armies, are near madness. Victory for either side can mean tragedy in their homes. For them, news of a fight anywhere is never good news. Everyone is coping with grief over the death, dismemberment, disease or imprisonment of a loved one.

The people are thinner. The food supply for rich and poor alike is greatly diminished. When Johnston's Confederates and Patterson's Union troops occupied the county, they numbered more than the normal population of the county. With twice the mouths to feed, everything was consumed by man and beast. During Patterson's occupation of Martinsburg, his mules and horses alone consumed ten tons of forage a day! Kitchen gardens and local farms manage to produce enough food to feed people, but just barely. Almost daily, some family leaves the area to find a place to live where they can get enough to eat.

With the telegraph lines dismantled and sent south and newspapers no longer publishing, Sarah knows that the most reliable news comes from riders who visit the town. The war is all the talk. The men of the lower Shenandoah Valley are said to be heading to Winchester from their summer camps at Fairfax Court House. Everyone prays that this rumor is true. Since the battle at Manassas, both armies withdrew their concentrations of troops from the lower valley leaving the people in a dangerous "no man's land." With the militia and the armies removed from the area, the women, children and the elderly have no one to protect them from criminals who lurk in the shadows and strike the defenseless.

Some of the criminals are like debris, they seemed to have simply floated onto the southern shore of the Potomac River when the war began. Others are the familiar faces of county men who hide in the mountains to avoid being conscripted and survive by preying on the weak and defenseless.

The Harrison family, like most others, shutter their windows, lock their doors and outbuildings, hide their horses and sleep lightly every night. The slightest unusual sound is treated like it has the potential for mortal danger to the family. The night is a fearful time for everyone.

Sarah Harrison, not quite thirty years old, has suffered

greatly in the six short months since the war began. She knows she is not alone in her misery. Her circumstance is shared by her family, neighbors, friends and enemies. She has a strong belief in God to sustain her and an unshakable commitment to the cause that took her husband's life. She knows that somehow she grows stronger and more determined every day.

When she arises from the breakfast table, she wonders what the day will bring. She wonders if she has the strength to meet the day's challenges and dangers. She looks at her young children and knows that she is nearly alone in her responsibility to bring them safely through the war. As she touches the small gun hidden deeply in the folds of her skirt, she proudly lifts her chin and strides purposefully from the breakfast table. She has become a steely Confederate warrior, determined to win the life and death battles on the home-front. She has decided she will survive!

CANNON FIRE AT DAM NO. 5

In November 1861 the Confederate army returned to the lower Shenandoah Valley from its camps near the bloody battlefield at Manassas. The army had a new commander, the hero of Henry House Hill, "Stonewall" Jackson. The headquarters of the army was established at Winchester. This decision was made for practical reasons. Winchester was close enough to the Potomac River, the northernmost border of the South, to allow the army to picket and observe the movements of the enemy who was camped on the northern side of the river. The town was also far enough away from the border to give the Confederates time to prepare in the event that a Union force crossed the Potomac. The people of Winchester were grateful to live so far from the border and for the comforting protection the army would provide. The people of Berkeley, Jefferson and Morgan counties quickly realized that, once again, they would face any invading army with little protection. Such were the fortunes of war.

As the Panhandle men of the Confederate army began to slip home from the camps, their families were astonished at the changes in them. The men who returned were not the patriotic yet naive men who took the trains for Harpers Ferry half a year ago. They were thinner and more fit. The fancy uniforms and pompous trappings of militia men had been replaced by the practical equipage of warriors at arms. They were confident veterans of deadly encounters with the enemy. While they were affectionate and gentle with their families, they had a steely gaze in their eyes. They could tenderly bounce an infant on their knee in one moment or shoot the first thing that moved in the next.

The men were equally surprised at the changes in their families. The women and children had endured occupation. The women, who had once looked to their men for every decision and as their only means of safety, were more confident and assertive. The children were savvy. They had learned to protect themselves from hardened strangers with guns, to avoid thundering cavalry units and, when necessary, to stealthily take from unsuspecting Union troops what might be desperately needed by their families to survive.

Over supper tables, in moments of shared intimacy, families whispered their beliefs that not a moment should be wasted, that the enemy must be crushed quickly. All agreed that no effort or sacrifice was too much to reach victory. While families reassured their men they could survive, the soldiers assured loved ones their army would be victorious.

When they returned to their camps, the men were restless. They had learned that war was a matter of endless waiting punctuated only occasionally with terrifying yet thrilling encounters with the enemy. Their commanding general, "Stonewall" Jackson, was also impatient with camp life. He decided to take advantage of the relatively mild winter weather to make use of his army's energy and to strike yet another tactical blow at the Union. The east-west rail line between Baltimore and the Ohio Valley had been destroyed by his troops during the summer. The Chesapeake and Ohio Canal, along the northern side of the Potomac, was still operational and carrying critical supplies to the Union. Jackson determined to take his men to Berkeley County and to destroy the C & O Canal.

On December 7, Jackson led a contingent of his infantry troops and the Rockbridge Artillery with their six Parrot guns to Big Spring, a familiar camp outside of Martinsburg. There they left their baggage, tents and wagons before proceeding to Martinsburg. At Martinsburg, Jackson ordered Colonel Turner Ashby to have his cavalry command arrest all known disloyal persons in the Hedgesville-Little Georgetown area so that they could not cross the Potomac to inform the Union command of the Confederate movement toward the Potomac. In that roundup, Unionists Teeter M. French and John Harley Miller were dragged from their homes at Hedgesville and imprisoned in the city jail at Martinsburg.

Awaiting word from the cavalry that the arrests had

been completed, Confederate troops rested in downtown Martinsburg for a few hours, then marched 13 miles to the shore of the Potomac across from Dam No.5, seven miles west of Williamsport, and waited until darkness fell. Led by a respected Hedgesville native in the Second Virginia Infantry, Raleigh Colston, the men waded waist-deep into the frigid waters armed with shovels, axes, and battering hammers to force a breach in the dam.

Union troops on the northern shore had watched the Confederate troops positioning themselves and harassed them all day with sniper fire. The Confederates covered the work on the dam with cannon fire. At the first sound of cannon, skirmishing erupted between pickets all along the river. At daylight, the Confederates withdrew.

That day, Union General Banks wired his superior General McClellen to alleviate panic in the North. He reassured the commanding General that Jackson was not occupying the border in force nor was he invading Maryland. Nevertheless, a large number of Union troops were dispatched to Williamsport to reinforce the guard along the Potomac from Harpers Ferry to Hancock. In response, Jackson sent the old and infirm men of the local militia to engage Union troops along the river from Falling Waters to Dam No.5. The troop buildup terrified local citizens who hurriedly evacuated their homes.

On December 11, Jackson sent a contingent to Dam No. 4 to confuse Union troops and draw their attention from the continuing work at Dam No. 5. The Confederates found that the Union troops had been reinforced and cannon were carefully "zeroed in" on their positions. Immediately fighting erupted at Dam No.4 and again the entire border resounded with the sounds of canon and small arms. The Confederates withdrew at daylight.

A week later the determined Jackson and his men returned to Dam No.5. The working parties were under constant heavy fire but continued to labor in the dark, freezing waters. Companies from the Thirty-third and Twenty-seventh Virginia Infantry persisted and that night created a breach large enough to render a stretch of the canal from Dam No. 4 to Dam No. 5 useless.

Men on both sides were grievously wounded and some were killed in the skirmishing over Dam No. 5. The most curiously wounded man was Private James Emswiller of Company "B", Seventh Virginia Cavalry. In the excitement of battle, a Union sniper failed to remove the ramrod from his gun before he fired. He aimed at Emswiller, pulled the trigger and the long metal shaft entered Emswiller's chin and exited his head above his eye. Large amounts of his brain matter exited with the ramrod. Surgeon Burns felt certain that the wound was fatal but the tough Emswiller recovered. For the remainder of his time with the Seventh, his comrades joked about his terrible wound by saying that they thought he had more sense after losing his brains than before!

Jackson's men continued their work on the canal until withdrawn on December 21. The breach in the canal had been costly in human suffering. Men were dead and wounded. Property in Berkeley County had been set afire in the cannon duels. People had fled from their homes into the bitter winter weather and suspected spies had been arrested. The breach in the canal was readily repaired by Union troops and canal traffic had been interrupted only briefly.

The operation at Dam No.5 had little military value but it served to remind the people of the border counties that neither winter weather nor the spirit of the Christmas season would spare them from the cruel realities of war. As Confederate families in Winchester, Richmond, and Atlanta lifted their cups to celebrate the birth of the Christ Child in the warmth and safety of their homes, the cold, hungry and frightened people of Berkeley, Jefferson and Morgan counties gathered their courage to survive yet another day.

BITTER COLD AND
BATTLE AT BATH

*"There were eleven of them. Some were sitting
down and some were lying down! But each and
every one was as cold and hard frozen as the icicles
that hung from their hands, faces and clothing —
dead! They had died at their post of duty."*

*-Sam Watkins in Company Aytch
regarding the 14th Georgia Infantry
at Sir John's Run, January 4, 1862*

As Confederate General "Stonewall" Jackson and
his army of 8,500 freezing troops approached Berkeley
Springs on January 3, 1862, the Union army was firmly
in control of northern Morgan County, the Baltimore
and Ohio Railroad, the crossings of the Potomac River
and everything on the Maryland side of the river.

The Union troops patrolled the area under their control and maintained usual security measures but their
state of readiness for battle was relaxed. At the Alpine
Railroad Station, Bath, Hancock, Sir John's Run and
Great Cacapon, the troop's overwhelming concern was
staying warm in the hideously cold weather. They
doubted that even a small Confederate patrol would
approach them in such weather. The approach of an

entire army was unimaginable!

Jackson had a clear picture of the location of all the Union troops in the area. Spies and southern sympathizers had passed the word about the number of Union men, their arms and ammunition supply, their locations and their routines. Using this information, Jackson sent his men into northern Morgan County to attack Union strong points.

Confederate General Carson and his militia were sent into the area by a western route thorough Rocky Gap and down Sir John's Valley. Colonel Ashby and his cavalry were sent down the Martinsburg Road and ordered to enter Bath from the east. General Loring's command was to enter Bath via the Winchester Grade Road. In the late afternoon on January 3, nearby civilians heard the battle for Bath begin when gun fire erupted as leading troops from Loring's command encountered a Union cavalry patrol three miles from Bath and Carson's militia repulsed a Union advance west of Warm Spring Ridge.

The next morning, Jackson sent his regiments toward Bath along the mountain ridge east and west while Ashby's cavalry thundered into the town and routed the Union cavalry it found there, forcing them into a wild retreat toward Hancock.

The fighting seemed to be everywhere. The First Tennessee was ambushed with heavy fire by Federal Cavalry along the ridge above the town. Ashby's command overtook the rear guard of the Union Cavalry and fought them persistently during their retreat along the Hancock Road. When Confederate infantry followed the cavalry into the town, Union artillery on Warm Spring Ridge shelled the invading enemy as well as the civilians of the town. When the Confederates reached the river, Jackson ordered the enemy in Hancock shelled. At Sir John's Run, Confederates skirmished with retreating troops but failed to capture them. At Great Cacapon, Arkansas troops fought with Union troops in a bloody exchange.

On that first day of the "killing war" in Morgan County, Confederate troops had overwhelmed the Union army at Bath, Sir John's Run, Great Cacapon and Alpine Station. They had forced fifteen hundred Federals back toward safety across the Potomac at Hancock. As the sun set, the tired, cold and hungry Confederate troops filled the luxurious hotels of the resort town of Bath while the civilians crept cautiously from their homes to examine the bodies of dead men, horses and mules that lay along the roads near their homes.

Like their friends and relatives in Berkeley and Jefferson counties, the people of Morgan had now seen the ugly, terrifying and death-dealing side of war. No one would sleep well that night. Surrounded by more than eight thousand Confederate troops and trapped across the river from a growing body of Union troops, they prayed that they would survive the fighting that would surely come at day break.

"TELL JACKSON TO BOMBARD AND BE D——D!"

By dawn on January 5, 1862, General Jackson's Confederate troops had chased the Union army out of Morgan County. From the Maryland side of the Potomac, the men in blue could see the Confederate troops stationed menacingly on the bluffs opposite Hancock. Jackson's intention to take the Maryland town was obvious. While men on both sides of the river nervously fingered their weapons and awaited the coming battle, civilians gathered in small, frightened groups wondering what might happen next.

Shortly, a white flag was raised by the Confederate troops, indicating they wanted to communicate with the leader of the Union force at Hancock. Lt. Colonel O.L. Mann of the Thirty-Ninth Illinois Infantry, appointed Provost Marshall of Hancock just that morning, was ordered to take a small detachment across the river to receive the communication. He was astonished to meet the famous, dashing cavalry officer, Colonel Turner Ashby. Ashby was to deliver the communication personally to Union commander.

Mann blindfolded Ashby so that he could learn nothing of the troop and artillery concentrations in the town and took him directly to the hard-drinking, well respected explorer, Brigadier General Frederick West Lander. At forty-one, Lander was a veteran of five cross country trips as an explorer for the transcontinental railroad and a tough soldier. He had been seriously wounded in the fall and had recently taken command of his division although his wound had not healed.

Lander received Colonel Ashby in the telegraph office but moved their meeting to another room fearing that the cavalry officer might understand the incoming messages. Ashby's blindfold was removed and he presented General Jackson's letter.

Jackson demanded the surrender of all Union forces under Lander's command. He said he had fifteen thousand men and he planned to cross the river and take Hancock by force. Unless Lander surrendered, Jackson planned to prepare Hancock for the southern invasion by shelling the town. He gave Lander two hours to evacuate the civilians.

Lander's immediate response was characteristic of the man. He said, "Give my compliments to General Jackson and tell him to bombard and be d....d! If he opens his batteries on this town he will injure more of his friends than he will of the enemy for this is a d....d secesh place anyway!"

Ashby was returned to the Virginia side of the Potomac and gave Lander's response to Jackson. Word of the surrender demand spread through Hancock and civilians deserted the town. As Jackson waited the promised two hours, he was approached by loyal southerners who lived nearby. The ladies of the Swann and Orrick families told Jackson of the large number of Confederate civilians living in Hancock and begged him not to shell the town. After their visit, Jackson received reports of a large body of Union troops heading toward Hancock to reinforce Lander.

As the given time to surrender expired, defiant troops in the Thirty-Ninth Illinois raised their regimental flag on a pole that was visible to the Confederates. The Confederate cannons roared and were answered by the Union guns. For an hour an artillery duel plastered the landscape with deadly shot and shell. Then it was over. Jackson gave the order to move away from the river. He ordered his army to march toward Romney.

As the Confederate army moved out of Morgan County, the people who remained behind were stunned. Just days before, all they had known of war had been hot-headed talk, benign occupation, petty arrests and incessant demands for a loyalty oath from both sides. Now they, too, had "seen the elephant." They had seen the horror of war and felt the terror of death lurking just outside their windows.

The county was in disarray. Terrified women had given birth to their babies prematurely. Some of the elderly with heart conditions lay dying from the stress. Every window in any home unfortunate enough to have been near the fire of an artillery battery had been shattered. The railroad had been torn up, all the railroad property had been burned. Unionist homes had been ransacked and burned to the ground. Many homes and buildings had been repeatedly pierced by cannon balls and bullets. Dead men in shallow graves were strewn throughout the countryside along with dead horses and mules.

While the people of Winchester and the rest of the upper Shenandoah Valley continued to talk of war and bake bread for the soldiers, the people in Morgan County joined their neighbors from Berkeley and Jefferson counties in the sad fraternity of civilians who had been caught in the cross fire of a war not yet nine months old. The terror, the horror and the wanton destruction moved them to pray that war would never pass their way again.

KNOWN SKIRMISHES
IN BERKELEY, JEFFERSON
AND MORGAN COUNTIES
APRIL 1861 - JANUARY 1862

<u>1861</u>

April 18	Abandonment of Harpers Ferry
May 17	Skirmish at McCoy's Ferry
May 23	Skirmish at McCoy's Ferry
June 2	Skirmish at Lemen's Ferry
June 15	Evacuation of Harpers Ferry
	Skirmish at Falling Waters
June 24	Skirmish at Falling Waters
July 2	Skirmish at Lemen's Ferry
	Action at Falling Waters
July 4	Skirmish at Harpers Ferry
July 11	Skirmish at Martinsburg
July 15	Skirmish at Darkesville
	Action at Bunker Hill
July 16	Picket Affair at Charles Town
July 18	Skirmish near Bunker Hill
July 21	Skirmish at Charles Town
Sept. 9	Skirmish at Shepherdstown
Sept. 17	Skirmish at Harpers Ferry
Oct. 11	Skirmish at Harpers Ferry
Oct. 16	Action at Bolivar Heights
Dec. 7	Skirmish at Dam #5 on the C&O Canal
Dec. 8	Skirmish at Dam #5

Dec. 11	Skirmish at Dam #4
Dec. 12	Skirmish at Scrabble
Dec. 17	Skirmish at Dam #5
Dec. 18	Skirmish at Dam #5
	Skirmish at Falling Waters
Dec. 19	Skirmish at Dam #4
	Skirmish at Falling Waters
Dec. 20	Sskirmish at Dam #5
	Skirmish at Falling Waters
	Skirmish at Little Georgetown
Dec. 22	Skirmish at Little Georgetown
Dec. 25	Skirmish at Cherry Run

1862

January 3	Skirmish near Bath
January 4	Skirmish at Bath
	Skirmish along the Hancock Road
	Skirmish at Great Cacapon
	Skirmish at Alpine Depot
January 5	The Shelling of Hancock
	Skirmish at Alpine Depot
	Skirmish at Great Cacapon

THE MEN FROM THE LOWER SHENANDOAH VALLEY WHO FOUGHT IN THE CIVIL WAR: BERKELEY COUNTY

The people vast majority of men from the Lower Shenandoah Valley who fought in the Civil War were in the Confederate Army. In many families every man enlisted. In the cities, there were many blocks where every home contributed a Confederate soldier to the cause and in the country, adjacent farms that streched for miles gave their sons, brothers and fathers.

Every man who serves his country in any war derserves to be honored for his patriotism and sacrifice. This is certainly true of the men who fought for the North or the South in the Civil War. In many places in our country, their service is remembered with statues, memorial plaques and carefully preserved lists, unit histories and archives devoted to the preservztion of the memory of local men who bravely served in the war.

The men who fought from Berkeley, Jefferson and Morgan counties have not received those honors. Complete and accurate lists of thier names and thier wartime activities were not compiled and do not exist. Local histories contain a few names but the lists were compiled decades after the war and are full of errors and ommissions.

It is apalling to read through these histories and to find only a man's last name and a terse entry that he was killed. That man died for his country and had loved ones who grieved. Sadder still, that man may have descendants who are alive today and unaware of the his sacrifce.

With that in mind, I have made determined attempt to identify the men of the lower Shenandoah Valley who fought in the Civil War. I have reviewed thousands of Combined Service Records at the National Archives in Washington, D.C. , advertised widely in the local print media and on the Internet for inforamtion regarding these men., reviewed regimental histories, war time newspapers, post-war obituaries, cemetary records, Court House records and more.

Whenever possible I have a date and place of birth, occupation, family number in the 1850 or 1860 Census, the Combined Service Record, date of death and place of burial for these men.

The lists I have developed are extensive and space limitations dictate that I cannot include the names of all the men who fought from Berkeley, Jefferson and Morgan counties in this volume. Instead, I have included the men of Berkeley County in this volume and will include the names of the men of Jefferson County in Volume Two. The men from Morgan County will appear in Volume Three.

The following men are from **BERKELEY COUNTY**, West Virginia. When most enlisted, Berkeley County was in the Commonwealth of Virginia and, therefore, Confederate troops served in Virginia regiments.

The Berkeley men who fought for the Union served primarily in West Virginia units. The exception are the sixty-odd men who were recruited by Ward Hill Lamon, a Berkeley County man who became President Abraham Lincoln's law partner and body guard. These men were recruited into a unit known as the 1st Virginia Union Volunteers. This unit existed for only a short period of time. When it was disbanded the men were assigned to Pennsylvania and Maryland regiments.

No Union companies were organized in Berkeley County. Six Confederate companies were organized in Berkeley County and at the time of thier organization were filled entirely by men from the county.

The Units From Berkeley County

Company "B", 1st Regiment, (Pendelton's)Virginia Light Artillery, C.S.A.

This unit was originally known as the Ephraim G. Alburtis Battery, Virginia Light Artillery. It was organized at Martinsburg on Nov 19, 1859 immediately after

John Brown's Raid at Harpers Ferry. The first section of the battery was stationed at Charles Town during the execution of John Brown. With Ephraim G. Alburtis as its Captain, the unit was enrolled April 19, 1861 at Martinsburg for one year as Company "B", 1st Virginia Artillery. It was armed with four six-pound, smoothbore cannon on July 21, 1861. Alburtis resigned Jan. 25, 1862.

Captain James S. Brown took command of the unit on February 1, 1862. The unit was reorganized as an independent battery April 26, 1862 as (Captain James S.) Brown's Battery Light Artillery. It was armed with two twelve-pound howitzers and two six-pound Smoothbores in June and July 1862. on October 8, 1862, per Special Order No. 209, the artillery unit was disbanded, with most of the men assigned to the Captain John Lewis Eubank's/Osmond B. Taylor's Battery, Virginia Light Artillery, The Alburtis Artillery fought in twenty-three battles from 1st Manassas through the surrender at Appomattox.

Company "B"
1st Virginia Cavalry Regiment, C.S.A.

This unit was originally known at the Berkeley Troop. It was organized in Martinsburg in 1860. With Martinsburg attorney, John Blair Hoge, as its Captain, the company enlisted for active service at Martinsburg on April 19, 1861. Hoge resigned in August 1861. Captain George Newkirk Hammond, also of Berkeley County, took command following Hoge's resignation. This unit was one of 12 companies that comprised the 1st Virginia Cavalry. The first Virginia was commanded by Colonel. James Ewell Brown Stuart. The 1st Virginia Cavalry fought in 36 battles from Falling Waters on July 2, 1861 through the surrender at Appomattox Court House.

Companies "D" and "E"
2d Virginia Infantry
"The Stonewall Brigade"

Company "D" was originally known as the "Berkeley Border Guards". This militia company was organized 10/31/59 at Martinsburg following John Brown's raid at Harpers Ferry as part of the 67th Virginia Militia. It was on duty at Charles Town 3/16/60 at the hanging of John Brown. With John Quincy Adams Nadenbousch as its Captain, it was first ordered into state service by Virginia Governor Letcher on the night of April 18, 1861. The original company members were mustered into the Confederate army May 11, 1861. This company suffered more causalities than any other company in the Stonewall Brigade.

Company "E" was originally known as the "Hedgesville Blues." This militia company was organized at Hedgesville in the fall of 1861 following John Brown's Raid at Harpers Ferry as part of the 67th Virginia Militia. With Raleigh T. Colston as its Captain, it was first ordered into state service by Virginia Governor Letcher on the night of April 18, 1861. The original company members were mustered into the Confederate army May 11-12, 1861.

The Stonewall Brigade fought in forty-five battles and campaigns and Companies "D" and "E" surrendered at Appomattox.

Company "A"
17th Virginia Cavalry

This unit was originally known as the "Wildcat Company" and was organized October 7, 1861 at Martinsburg by Captain George W. Meyers After its organization, the Wildcat Company was stationed at Martinsburg, where its men were employed as pickets until late February 1862. Then they moved to Winchester, Strasburg and Woodstock taking part in most of Jackson's Valley Campaign, as part of Ashby's Cavalry. The Wildcat Company was reorganized April 23, 1862 at Conrad's Store. George W. Meyers was again elected Captain. After Turner Ashby's death, the Company was assigned to the 11th Virginia Cavalry in February 1863 per Special Order No. 36. This unit fought in numerous battles from the Wilderness through Early's Shenandoah campaign. No members of this unit surrendered at Appomattox.

Company "H"
27th Virginia Infantry

This unit was originally known as the "Dominion Grays" and mustered in at Darkesville on 4/19/61 and disbanded on June 10, 1861 because it failed to recruit enough men to fill a minimum sized company. There were sixty-seven men in this company. Most of these men joined other Berkeley County infantry units.

Companies "A" through "E"
67th Regiment Virginia Militia

Commanded by Jacob Sencidiver, this regiment was activated early June 1861 and dismissed June 14, 1861. It was composed entirely of men from Berkeley County. This regiment was again called out by the proclamation of the governor dated July 13, 1861. Five companies, "A" to "E" were in active service from August 10, 1861 to April 10, 1862 when the regiment was disbanded. Stationed at Camp Evans near Winchester, Va, the unit participated in the November 1861 skirmish at Sir John's Run, the December 1861 attempt to break Dam No.5 and related skirmishing, the January 1862 Bath/Romney campaign, and the February 12, 1862 skirmish at Bloomery Gap. Many men served in the militia and enlisted in other units of the Confederate army when the militia was disbanded. A few are known to have served in the militia and enlisted in Union companies when the militia was disbanded.

THE CONFEDERATE TROOPS AND MILITIA FROM BERKELEY COUNTY

Albin, James B.
Albin, Michael Harvey
Albritton, John T.
Alburtis, E. Gaither
Alburtis, Samuel
Allison, John
Allison, John H.
Ambrose, Christian
Ambrosia, Henry
Amey, William F.
Anderson, Eli
Anderson, James V.
Anderson, James W.
Anderson, John D.
Ardinger, Harry
Ardinger, John Percy
Armpriest, Jerome B.
Armstrong, John S.
Armstrong, J. William
Ashley, R.
Auld, Charles S.
Auld, Thomas Edward
Austin, John Thomas
Austin, William
Bain, F. M.
Bain, Issac Newton

Bain, Robert N.

Baker, Newton D.

Bales, Adam S.

Bales, David

Balous, W.H.

Barnes, Lemuel

Barnett, Andrew J.

Barnett, Josiah

Barr, George

Bartholow, Joshua

Bartholow, O. William

Basore, Emanuel

Basore, John Wesley

Beall, Alfred F.

Beall, Richard Harrison

Bear, John

Beard, George W.

Bechtel, John M.

Bell, Henry

Bender, A.

Bender, David

Bender, G.W.

Bender, Henry

Bender, Samuel

Benson, Joseph A.

Bentz, William T.

Berry, George.

Betz, James

Billmeyer, B.L.

Billmeyer, Milton J.

Billmeyer, Robert L.

Billmire, James

Bishop, L.D.

Bishop, Thomas Jefferson

Blake, Peter W.

Blake, Van Buren

Blakeney, David Harrison

Blakeney, Edward F.

Blakeney, George W.

Blamer, James W.

Blanchfield, John

Blondel, John H.

Blondell, Charles E.

Boak, J. Seibert

Bodine, John T.

Boley, Benjamin F.

Boltz, David M.

Boltz, George F.

Boltz, James

Bowers, D.

Bowers, F. M.

Bowers, John E.

Bowers, John W.

Bowers, Richard H.

Bowers, Theodore Frank

Bowen, Wilhelm

Boyd, Benjamin Reed

Boyd, John Elisha Jr.

Boyer, John A.
Brady, B.F.
Brady, Peter
Brandon, Thomas
Breathed, James W.
Bricker, Levi
Bristor, J.H.
Britner, Thaddeus Steven
Britton, Edward P.
Brocius, William
Brosnehan, Patrick
Brotherton, Robert R.
Brown, Charles J.
Brown, E.M.
Brown, Isaiah
Brown, James S.
Bryarly, Robert P.
Buchanan, John Charles
Buchanan, Thomas E.
Burch, George
Burke, Stephen A.
Burkhart, John D.
Burkhart, R. Christopher
Burnes, John
Burns, Issac Jr.
Burr, Frank A.
Buser, Theodore
Butler, John S.
Butler, John T.

Butler, John Thomas
Butts, David
Butts, Michael
Butts, Thomas Jefferson
Butts, William
Butts, William H.
Byrd, Derrick William
Cage, James D.
Cage, Richard
Callahan, James W.
Callahan, Samuel
Callen, Cornelius V.M.
Carlisle, James A.
Carney, Jacob V.
Carper, Jacob
Carper, John
Carter, George S.
Carter, James Pendelton
Caskey, William L.
Catow, John William
Cesimini, Giancinto
Chambers, George H.
Chambers, James H.
Chambers, John M.
Chambers, Robert D.
Chamblin, James E.
Chapman, Frank P.
Chapman, George Suel
Chapman, Jacob W.

Chapman, James W.
Chapman, Thomas J.
Charlton, George Bernard
Chenowith, Charles B.
Chenowith, George C.
Chenowith, James W.
Chevally, Samuel
Claiborb, George
Clary, T.V.
Clendening, A.
Clendening, Boyd
Clendening, William Coe
Cline, David Aaron
Cline, Henry
Cline, John W.
Cline, William Henry.
Coats, Jesse J.
Coats, Thomas D.
Cockran, Charles C.
Colbert, George A.
Colston, Edward H.
Colston, Raleigh Thomas
Colston, William B.
Combs, J.L.E.
Compton, George W.
Conrad, Henry Tucker
Conrad, Holmes Addsion
Conway, James
Copenhaver, Jacob D.

Couchman, David C.
Couchman, George W.
Couchman, Jacob Rush
Cox, Henry
Cox, Henry H.
Cox, Solomon
Coyle, Jerome B.
Coyle, Joseph C.
Crabb, William
Craftt, William
Crane, George W.
Crane, Willis
Crim, George W.
Crim, John W.
Criswell, John L.
Cross, Daniel W.
Cross, John
Cross, John Alexander
Cross, John E.
Cumiskey, Thomas
Cunningham, Charles A.
Cunningham, David P.
Cunningham, J. Newkirk
Cunningham, John A.
Cunningham, John F.
Cunningham, Phillip S.
Cunningham, William L.
Curtis, Philimon C.
Cushwa, David

Cushwa, Daniel G.
Custer, Ephraim Gaither
Dandridge, Edmund P.
Daniels, Robert
Davis, Benjamin D.
Davis, Joseph N.
Davis, L.M.
Davis, Samuel
Dawson, Thomas J.
Day, James W.
Dean, James W.
Deck, D. Morgan
Deck, Edward C.
Deck, Jacob H.
Deller, John O.
Dellinger, Frederick
Denner, John
Denny, James Hall
Derbing, Charles L.
Derry, Peter
Detter, John L.
Dieffenderfer, Bernard
Dilly, John R.
Dishman, William N.
Doll, Richard McSherry
Dorr, William T.
Dorsey, William Henry
Dugan, James F.
Dugan, James W.

Dugan, John A.
Dunham, Francis C.
Dunn, John
Earsome, Joseph B.
Ebberly, Daniel
Edwards, William H.
Eichelberger, D. Smith
Ellis, Ellis
Englebright, John H.
Entler, J.H.
Everhard, Ryneal
Eversole, J.H.
Eversole, John William
Eversoll, Issac H.
Eversoll, Jacob T.
Farris, Moses H.
Faulkner, Charles James
Faulkner, Charles James II
Faulkner, Elisha Boyd
Feaman, James
Fiery, James Van
Files, John B.
Finucan, John P.
Finucan, Patrick
Fiser, John L.
Fisher, James W.
Fisher, John L.
Fiske, James
Flagg, Thomas G.

Foreman, Jacob J.
Foreman, P.J.
Foreman, Perry Jacob
Fowler, Samuel P
Fravel, George W.
Frazier, James W. B.
Freeze, Andrew Jackson
Freeze, George F.
Fritz, John
Fritz, Thomas
Fryatt, D.W.
Fryatt, George W.
Fryatt, James
Fryatt, John Tillotson
Frye, Atwell Washington
Frye, Issac
Fultz, Thornton
Fuss, J. Frederick
Gageby, John N.
Gallagher, J. Columbus
Gallagher, Patrick
Gano, James W.
Gardner, Jervus S.
Gauve, James
Gladden, George
Gladden, T. Seibert
Glass, Greenburg
Goheen, Michael
Gold, Samuel

Gordon, John D.
Gore, George
Gore, Norval
Gorrell, Joseph C.
Graves, Richard P.
Graves, William C.
Gray, James W.
Gregory, George W.
Griffin, Michael
Griffith, Johnson William
Griffith, Morris
Gruber, Josiah
Guin, John William
Guinn, J. Martin Van B.
Haines, John Jonas
Hall, Jugartha G.
Hamilton, William L.
Hammil, J. Alexander
Hammond, G. Newkirk
Harddox, William
Hardy, George William
Hardy, James Arthur
Hardy, Joseph
Harlan, George Boyd
Harlan, J. Wilkerson
Harlan, Silas George
Harlan, William Hunter
Harley, Patrick
Harman, William A.

Harrison, James P.
Harrison, John S.
Harrison, P. Randolph
Harrison, Samuel P.
Hartley, James W.
Hayden, James E.
Hays, James Franklin
Hays, Samuel
Hazard, Charles
Hedges, Anthony
Hedges, Bailey Seaton
Hedges, Decatur
Hedges, Ephraim Gaither
Hedges, Owen Tudor
Hedges, Samuel
Hedges, Theodore F.
Hefferstine, Richard M.
Helvestry, William R.
Hensell, Edward
Hensell, John S.
Hensell, Robert Scott
Hensell, William J.
Henshaw, James William
Henshaw, Marion Lee
Herbert, Zephania
Hess, Aaron T.
Hess, Charles M.
Hess, George
Hess, John

Hess, Joseph Francis
Hess, Solomon
Hetzel, Frederick
Hill, Abraham
Hill, Christopher
Hill, Joseph G.
Hill, M.E.
Hill, Martin Luther
Hill, Michael
Hill, William John
Hinds, John M.
Hite, Jackson
Hodges, Issac N.
Hoffman, Edmund Lee
Hoge, John Blair
Hollida, John M.
Hollida, John Wesley
Hollis Thomas W.
Hollis, John A.
Hollis, Thomas P.
Homrick, James H.
Hooper, Edward B.
Hout, William N.
Howard, Lemuel
Hughes, Andrew Jackson
Hughes, Smith M..
Hull, Dallas S.
Hull, George M..
Hull, John T.

Hull, Welcome
Hunter, David B.
Hunter, John Abell
Hunter, John C.
Hunter, Robert Adell
Hunter, Robert Waterman
Hutchinson, Samuel
Irdella, John Andria
Irdella, Michael
Isreal, Gilbert T.
Janney, Aquilla
Janney, William Henry H.
Jefferson, William Meade
Jenkins, Asa
Jenkins, George
Johnson, Abraham
Johnson, Issac
Johnson, William
Johnston, William
Jones, Hiram S.
Jones, W.J.
Jordon, H. William
Jordon, John
Joy, John F.
Joy, John T.
Joy, John W.
Kearfott, James Lemen
Kearfott, John Piercell
Kearfott, Peter R.

Kearfott, W. Pierceall
Kearns, Cyrus McLean
Kearns, Joseph
Kearns, Richard
Keefe, John William
Kees, John H.
Keesecker, George
Keesecker, Issac Newton
Keiter, W. William
Kensel, Henry
Kensel, John James
Kerfoot, Azariah
Kerfoot, Henry
Kerfoot, James M.
Kerns, George M.
Kibler, William H.
Kilmer, Barnet S.
Kilmer, David
Kilmer, George W.
Kilmer, Harrison, P.
Kilmer, John Daniel
Kilmer, William
King, Oliver
Kiser, Isaiah
Kiser, John B.
Kisner, G. Washington
Kisner, George William
Kisner, Henry
Kisner, John Q. Adams

Kisner, Joseph
Kisner, William
Kisner, William H.
Kitchen, George W.
Kitchen, John M.
Koontz, Francis
Koontz, Thornton
Kreglow, George T.
Kreglow, Jacob R.
Lambert, Albert R.
Lambert, Charles O.
Landers, Michael Dennis
Lanham, Jeremiah
Lantz, Christian Sr.
Lantz, Christian Jr.
Lantz, John
Lantz, Joseph T. Van
Larkins, Thomas
Lashorn, Jacob V.
Lashorn, William R.
Lawyer, Adam
Leach, Sidney
Leathers, John Hess
Lehand, John
Lemen, Hiram H.
Lemon, William M.
Lemon, Wyncoop
Lewis, David
Lewis, Franklin

Lewis, Jacob
Lewis, John
Lewis, Lewis
Lewis, Walter
Light, Edward
Light, John M..
Light, Joseph
Light, William E.
Light, William H.
Light, William K.
Light, William R.
Lingamfelter, Walter H.
Linton, Alex
Linton, John Manning
Little, Edward Vincent
Lockhart, C.E.
Lowman, James L.
Lowry, Benjamin William
Lowry, Robert
Lucas, Benjamin
Lucas, Charles W.
Lucas, Edward D.
Lucas, George B.
Lucas, Oscar M.
Lucas, Robert Rion
Lupton, Martin C.
Lupton, Thomas D.
Lyle, Robert Glen
MacDonald, Walter

Mahoney, Patrick
Mallory, T.D.
Manor, Charles W.
Manor, David H.
Markle, George W.
Markle, John B.
Markle, Joseph Smith
Markle, Samuel
Markle, Thomas P.
Marshall, George W.
Marshall, James A.
Marshall, Joseph E.
Mason, James B.
Mathews, Henry C.
Mauck, Daniel
Maupin, Algernon Tyre
Maxwell, John
May, John H.
McBee, William H.
McBee, William T.
McCleary, G. William
McCoy, P.J.
McDaniel, John P.
McDonald, Enos
McDonald, Walter J.
McDonald, William
McGarey, William H.
McIntire, John F.
McIntire, Richard W.

McKee, Mayberry
McKeever, Asa
McKinney, F.E.
McKown, Benjamin W.
McLaughlin, Francis
McLaughlin, Franklin
McMullen, Lambert G.
McNamara, Michael
McPhillen, J.
McSherry, James Whann
McSherry, Richard M.
McWhorter, James N.
Meachem, Richard
Merchant, Sewell
Merchant, Washington
Merk, Thomas
Meyers, Benjamin
Meyers, Jacob
Meyers, James
Meyers, W.H.
Miller, George W.
Miller, Harvey Allen
Miller, Henry
Miller, Henry C.
Miller, J.E.
Miller, John A.
Miller, Jonathan
Miller, Joseph
Miller, Samuel S.

Minghini, Charles L.
Minghini, Joseph Lee
Mingle, John A.
Minor, Reuben T
Mix, George
Moler, Raleigh
Mong, George Ramer
Mong, Wendell
Montague, Lawrence A.
Moody, John P.
Mooney, John B.
Moore, Andrew M.
Moore, Joseph
Morris, Layton B.
Mullen, Henry W.
Mullen, Samuel
Mulligan, James
Mulligan, John Patrick
Murphy, George H.
Murphy, Patrick
Murphy, Richard Davis
Murray, Henry
Murray, Patrick
Myers, Aaron
Myers, Cromwell
Myers, George W.
Myers, James W.
Myers, John W.
Myers, William

Nadenbousch, John Q. A.
Nicholson, Edward Jr.
Nicholson, Thomas A.
Noland, William L.
Noll, William T.
O'Brien, Thomas
O'Byrnes, W.E.
O'Conner, Michael
O'Conner, Patrick
O'Neal, John R.
O'Conner, Michael
Oden, Archibald
Page William M..
Page, Richard L.
Page, Thomas D.
Page, William Byrd
Painter, Joseph M.
Painter, Richard McSherry
Palmer, William Kearny
Pare, James
Parker, Thomas S.
Patterson, Frank
Patterson, James
Patterson, John W.
Payne, John Summerfield
Payne, Martin Long
Payne, Orrick F.
Payne, Thomas
Pendleton, Charles Mason

Pendleton, Phillip Clayton
Perejoy, Edwin C.
Perejoy, William R.
Phillips, William
Piet, A.M..
Pike, Francis
Piper, John R.
Pitzer, C.R.
Pitzer, Elias M..
Pitzer, George V.
Place, Joseph
Poisal, Jacob V.
Porterfield, Alexander R.
Porterfield, George A.
Porterfield, Jacob Milton
Potts, Joseph E.
Powell, Lewis S.
Prather, Denton
Pryor, John
Pryor, Thomas E.
Ramer, George S.
Randall, A.W.
Reafort, John P.
Reed, George W.
Reed, James F.
Reed, James M..
Rees, John H.
Reynolds, Daniel
Rice, James M.

Rice, John
Rice, Samuel
Rice, William T.
Richards, James W.
Riddle, John Nourse
Riddleberger, W. Joseph
Ridenour, George
Ridenour, Martin F.
Ridgeway, A. Jackson
Ridgeway, H.J.
Ridgeway, Josiah J.
Riley, Andrew
Riner, Daniel
Riordan, John Timothy
Roach, John
Robbins, James Allen
Roberts, George
Roberts, William H.
Robinson, George H.
Robinson, Isreal Jr.
Robinson, Isreal Sr.
Robinson, James W.
Robinson, John S.
Robinson, William
Rockwell, George W.
Rockwell, John
Rogers, Casper
Rogers, John P.G.
Rogers, Robert

Ronk, Martin Benton
Ropp, George H.
Ropp, J.S.
Rose, Augustus P.
Roush, Charles Martin
Roush, George Smith
Rush, William
Rust, William
Rutherford, George B.
Ryneal, Everhard
Ryneal, Frederick
Sales, Richard
Sales, William T.
Satterfield, Ephraim
Satterfield, John W.
Saville, Albert
Schaarman, Phillip
Seaman, Jonah
Seaman, Richard D.
Seckman, Benjamin
Seckman, David
Seckman, Thomas
Seibert, Abraham
Seibert, George W.
Seibert, John Beatty
Seibert, John Eli
Seibert, Joseph
Seibert, Wendell
Sencidiver, George

Sencidiver, George(2)
Sencidiver, J.L.
Sencidiver, Jacob Morgan
Sencidiver, J. Morgan
Sencidiver, Lewis M.
Sharff, Peter Nicholas
Shea, James
Shea, John
Shearer, George
Sheig, George
Sheig, Adolphus
Shepherd, John Newton
Shepherd, Robert
Shepherd, T.C.
Shepherd, William W.
Sherrard, John M.
Sherrard, William
Sherrard, William G.
Sherrer, Joseph E.
Shilling, Jacob R.
Shingelton, William W.
Shingluff, John
Shober, Charles
Showers, George Ezekiel
Showers, James M.
Shroad, Richard
Shull, Charles
Shultz, William
Siler, John W.

Silver, Francis III
Silver, Henry Clay
Silver, Zephaniah
Simmons, John H.
Simmons, Joseph C.
Simpson, Caleb Simon
Sisco, John E.
Sisco, Peter
Small, David H.
Small, David Mack
Small, James H.
Small, John M..
Small, John W.
Small, Mayberry Goheen
Small, Reuben W.
Small, William C.
Smeltzer, Charles W.
Smith, Boyd
Smith, Frank T.
Smith, George W.
Smith, Henry C.
Smith, James
Smith, John S.
Smith, William M.
Smith, William Dean
Smith, Zedekiah
Snodgrass, A. Porterfield
Snodgrass, Issac Breathed
Snodgrass, John B.

Snyder, James Allemong
Sperow, G.O.
Sperow, George T.
Sperow, Jacob T.
Staff, Albert W.
Staff, Charles E.
Staub, John F.
Staub, Richard Patrick H.
Stevens, Arthur
Stevens, Giles
Stewart, Barnet W.
Stewart, John M.
Stewart, John W.
Stewart, Joseph
Stewart, Robert
Stewart, Robert H.
Stine, Jonathan
Straney, Edward F.
Strayer, Daniel J.R.
Stribling, John Maxwell
Strode, Joseph S.
Strode, Parker
Strode, S.R.T.
Stuckey, Charles
Stuckey, Daniel
Stuckey, John W.
Stuckey, Samuel A.
Stump, Casper M.
Stump, John Henry

Sudduth, James Arthur
Suiter, Charles M..
Suiter, Thomas Charles
Sullivan, Daniel F.
Sullivan, Edward
Sutton, Charles H.
Sweeny, C. W.
Swimley, David
Swimley, Harrison H.
Swygart, Louis
Tabb, Charles Walker
Tabb, Edward Walker
Tabb, Harrison Noble
Tabler, Adam
Tabler, Ephraim Gaither
Tabler, Lewis E.
Tabler, Martin L.
Talbott, John
Taliaferro, Charles C.
Talley, Issac
Tate, Robert John
Thatcher, David M.
Thomas, Benjamin B.
Thompson, Abraham
Thompson, Samuel Jasper
Thornburg, Collins P.
Thornburg, Issac Newton
Thornburg, Millard
Throckmorton, W.W.

Thrush, John M..
Tinsman, Samuel
Titlow, Henry J.
Titlow, Robert
Turner, James D.
Turner, John A.
Turner, Magill
Turner, William
Vanmeter, Asahel Morgan
Vanmeter, Charles
Vanmeter, Issac
Vanmeter, James L. E.
Vanmeter, Joseph B.
Vogel, John A.
Voorhees, Abraham
Voorhees, George Frank
Voorhees, John
Wagely, William
Walker, Elias M.
Walker, George W.
Walker, James H.
Walther, Frederick
Wandling, Allan
Warton, Isreal
Warton, Issac
Warton, Nathaniel
Wason, John
Waters, James W.
Weaver, John

Webster, Richard A.

Weddel, George

Weddel, John H., Jr.

Weise, James E.

Welch, Charles A.

Welsh, William Clinton

Weller, Charles R.

Wells, George

Wentz, Henry D.

West , Charles

Westphall, Charles

Wever, Charles J.

Wever, David J.

Wever, George Lowery

White, Michael

Whitehurst, James

Whitmore, John G.

Whitson, George D.

Whittington, Charles R.

Wilburn, John

Wiley, John Bolling

Wills, Samuel M.

Wilson, J.J

Wilson, Jeremiah

Wilson, John Park

Wilson, Louis F.

Wilson, Valarius W.

Wilson, Walker

Wilt, John

Wintermeyer, Thomas S.

Wirt, Henry D.

Witherow, James

Wolfe, George A.

Wolfe, Jacob

Wolff, Bernard Likens

Wolff, William

Wollett, George

Young, John R.

UNION

Two companies in the Union army contained significant numbers of men from Berkeley County. They were:

Company "C"
Third WV Cavalry

Organized December 1863 at Charles Town in Jefferson County. It was said to have been composed of many men from Martinsburg and Berkeley County. It fought in 22 engagements. Among them are two were at Martinsburg, three at Bunker Hill, one at Darkesville, Hagerstown and Hancock.

Company "B"
1st Virginia Union Volunteers

This company was organized by Ward Hill Lamon at Williamsport, Md. Four companies (A, B C & I) were composed of Unionist Virginians, largely from Ohio River border counties in western Virginia, were organized at Williamsport from June 18, 1861 to February 17, 1862. At the time of its organization Company "B" was composed largely of Berkeley County and Morgan men. Its first service was guarding a wagon train to Martinsburg. It was transferred to the 3rd Maryland Infantry on 5/11/62 and re-designated Company "D".

It is important to note that the names of fifty-two of the men from this company are in the following list of Union troops from Berkeley County. The names were taken from a local history, "Aler's History of Martinsburg and Berkeley County" and are said to be Berkeley County men by the author. No public records in Berkeley County (marriage records, tax rolls, census rolls or cemetary lists) show that these men had any ties to Berkeley County before or after the war. It is likely that they were remembered as comrades-in-arms by Berkeley County veterans but were not Berkeley County men.

UNION TROOPS FROM BERKELEY COUNTY

Adams, George F.
Allison, John H.
Anderson, Eli
Anderson, James W.
Ashkettle, J.
Ball, John
Barnes, Lemuel
Bartholow, Joshua
Bartholow, O. William
Batch, C.
Bateman, C.
Baylor, Richard C.
Baylor, Robert William
Bechtol, Henry C.
Bender, John
Benson, Joseph A.
Bishop, John
Boarman, Charles
Booth, John
Bowers, John E.
Bowers, John T.
Bricker, Levi
Bristor, J.H.
Brown. Wilhelm
Burch, George
Burris, E.
Butler, John Thomas
Butts, David
Butts, William H.
Cann, John
Caskey, J.
Claspey, James
Cleary, J. Lewis
Clendening, William Coe
Clevinger, Franklin
Cline, John W.
Cochran, Charles C.
Cochran, Hiram
Colbert, George A.
Colbert, Jesse
Conger, Seymor B.
Coyle, James
Cross, John A.
Crowl, Joseph B.
Curry, Alonzo H.
Dailey, Joseph
Daniels, George
Davis, Arthur
Davis, Samuel Y.
Davis, Ulysses
Deen, George W.

Deets, James
Deets, William
Deniam, George
Dickerhoff, Issac
Dilly, John R.
Ditman, John
Dugan, Samuel W.
Ebough, James N.
Espenhaim, John G.
Fahey, Thomas
Falkenstein, John
Farris, John
Fayman, James D.
Ferrel, Michael
Finigan, John Patrick
Fitz, Frederick
Fitzpatrick, David
Fleming, William
Fravel, John
French, Teter M.
Friskey, Lewis B.
Frizer, John T.
Frushour, William A.
Gagle, John H.
Gallaher, Joshua S.
Gano, John W.
Gardner, John F.
Garrett, George
Giser, Christian

Goodman, John
Grace, Edward
Graves, Charles
Green, David S.
Green, Martin B.
Grindes, R.
Harker, Charles
Harmin, M. Hewitt
Harrison, J.H.
Harrison,   Napoleon
Bonaparte
Hart, Jacob H.
Hays, Joseph H.
Henlane, Henry
Henry, John W.
Henry, Levi
Hensell, P.H.
Hickman, Gilaspie
Hipper, A.
Hipper, John
Hodges, Willliam G.
Hoffman, John E.
Hoffman, William G.
Horner, Alexander
Horner, Edmund
Horner, Robert Greer
Hunter, E. Pendleton
Hutzler, James William
Hutzler, John Castleman

Ingless, Joseph
Ingram, John
Isreal, Edward
Jack, John C.
Jenkins, George
Johnson, George
Johnson, John
Johnson, William
Jones, James
Kearns, Joseph
Kilcross, John
Kilgore, C.
Kines, W.E.
Kiser, David
Kiser, Isaiah
Kiser, John D.
Kneadler, James William
Lamon, Ward Hill
Lazzel, William G.
Lemaster, John H.
Lemaster, Theodore M.
Light, Issac Joseph
Links, Henry
Lintcon, John C.
Long, George
Lowery, Benjamin
Lowery, Robert
Lowman, John
Loy, Edward N.

Lutman, Henry Daniel
Martin, Burelle
Martin, John
Mathews, Franklin
Mauk, James Monroe
McBee, Franklin
McBee, Harrison
McBee, Henry C.
McBee, William T.
McEntire, James
McKinney, Robert A.
Mercer, Marshall
Meyers, Isaac
Meyers, Samuel
Meyers, William C.
Meyers, William
Michael, Henry H.
Michael, Joseph
Miller, Levi F.
Moler, Samuel
Moreland, Basil
Morgan, Edmund
Morgan, Elijah
Morgan, Enoch
Morgan, Robert,
Murphey, James William
Murphey, Samuel E.
Murphy, Dennis
Murphy, John W.

Murray, Samuel E.

Myers, Enos

Myers, Jacob

Norris, Josephus

Novington, John W.

Orman, John Norington

Parnpell, Jerome E.

Pendleton, Edmund

Perry, James

Perry, James S.

Pitzer, Charles W.

Pitzer, John W.

Poisal, Adam S.

Porter, Alfred

Potter, Noah

Prescott, Benjamin F.

Price, George L.

Price, Van A.

Prossman, William

Pullin, William

Racey, Westpol

Ramsburg, Elijah

Rathman, George V.

Richards, Issac

Ridenour, James

Ridenour, Charles

Ridgeway, Sylvester

Roach, James

Roach, Joseph

Roby, Middelton

Ross, James O.

Sadler, John

Shaffer, Balser

Shaffer, David

Shank, Samuel

Shaw, William

Shipley, William

Shirk, Jacob

Shrout, Andrew J.

Siler, Phillip

Sisco, John

Sisco, Joseph

Slater, Henry M.

Smith, David

Smith, John E.M.

Smith, Mathias

Smith, William M.

Spencer, Franklin

Spiker, William R.

St. Clair, James P.

Stafford, John

Stansburry, H.R.

Statler, Andrew J.

Statler, Henry M.

Statter, Benjamin F.

Stoker, Thomas

Strother, David H.

Strausbough, Harrison

Strawson, H.W.
Street, William J.
Tabler, John A.
Tabler, Peter
Tabler, William Murphey
Taylor, Ephraim
Taylor, James G.
Taylor, Samuel H.
Teets, Albert
Teets, Elisha
Teets, John
Thompson, Robert S.
Thompson, Samuel S.
Unger, John
Unger, Nicholas

Vanarsdale, Jeremiah
Vanmeter, Issac David
Wagely, Edmund H.
Walgamott, Moses
Weaver, David J.
Welsh, Patrick
Welsh, Thomas, S.
Welshans, Levi J.
Wharton, Fielding
Widmeyer, Samuel S.
Wise, Thomas
Wistar, Benjamin K.
Wolfe, Adam S.
Woodward, Charles W.
Yoho, Ezra

Berkeley County Men Who Are Known
To Have Fought - Affiliation Unknown

Barnwell, Stephen B.
Bittinger, Harry L.
Broghton, Walter N.
Broughton, Walter
Brown, D.D.
Campbell, David
Carnwell, Stephen B.
Carpenter, W.E.
Davis, George
Dettmer, George
Drenner, David F.
Drenner, John H.
Eagan, J. Patrick
Fitzgerald, Michael
Fraley, Daniel
Grozinger, John
Haddox, W.H.
Jacobs, Thomas R.
Kanter, William H.
Keedy, Walter H.
Knaggs, Joseph
Knipe, George W.
Mathers, Benjamin F.
McDowell, Charles
Miller, Stephen

Neville, Michael Henry
Riser, Hamilton
Ross, Daniel D.
Russler, A.T.
Shipman, John M.
Smaltz, Adam H.
Troxell, E.S.
Watson, Thomas
Wayble, Cyrus H.
Wells, Patrick Henry
Westrader, William
Williams, Alex

If you would like to know more about your Confederate ancestor who appears on this list of men from Berkeley County who fought in the Civil War, contact the author at P.O. Box 1851, Martinsburg, WV.

Glimpses of The Civil War in the Lower Shenandoah Valley: 1862-63 will contain a complete listing of men from **Jefferson County** who fought in the Civil War. This book will be available in May 1987.

SOURCES

The history of the Civil War in the Berkeley, Jefferson and Morgan counties has not been carefully preserved in a single repository. Information about what happened in the area can be found in hundreds of locations and from innumerable sources. Piecing the story together requires the skills of a patient researcher and the instincts of a detective.

To date, more than 50,000 books have been written about the Civil War. Sadly, very few are about the events that took place in Berkeley, Jefferson and Morgan counties. For those who would like to learn more about the war in the area, there follows an overview of the sources I have found most helpful.

There are several published references that are essential to a basic understanding of the Civil War in the lower Shenandoah Valley. These are the *War of the Rebellion: Official Records of the Union and Confederate Armies* by the United States War Department, *The Southern Historic Society Papers* by the Society, *A Compendium of the War of the Rebellion* by Frederick H. Dyer, *Units of the Confederate States Army* by Joseph H. Crute, *Compendium of the Confederate Armies* by Stewart Sifakis, the *Virginia Regimental*

History Series published by Harold E. Howard, *The Civil War Day By Day* by E.B. Long and the *Civil War Dictionary* by Mark Boatner.

The manuscripts and Special Collections at the United States Army Military History Institute in Carlisle, Pennsylvania, and at the Library of Congress in Washington, D.C. are important repositories of original documents and personal papers of lower Shenandoah Valley citizens. The National Archives in Washington, D.C., maintains an enormous body of information about the Civil War and lower Shenandoah Valley information is available from numerous record groups. The Combined Service records of Union and Confederate volunteer soldiers who served during the Civil War and local defense forces, statements given to the Southern Claims Commission, records of civilian arrests, tax records, census records, Quartermaster records, maps and much more provide very specific detail of war-time life, people and events.

The traditional local references are *Aler's History of Martinsburg and Berkeley County West Virginia* by F. Vernon Aler, *Chronicles of Old Berkeley* by Mabel Henshaw Gardiner and her daughter, Ann Henshaw Gardiner, *History of Berkeley County* by Willis F. Evans, *Historic Jefferson County* by Millard K. Bushong, *Military Operations in Jefferson County* by Robert Preston Chew, and *Warm Springs Echoes* by

Frederick T. Newbraugh. These books provide general information on the history and culture of the area as well as specific information about the Civil War.

Historic Society information augments these traditional resources. Marriage and cemetary records, historic society magazines and booklets, genealogical files, Civil War-era newspapers on microfilm and much more are critical resources.

In addition to these, the civil war-era papers, diaries, letters and notes of Susan Nourse Riddle, Aaron T. Hess, John Quincy Adams Nadenbousch, Alexander R. Boteler, Charles James Faulkner, John Pendleton Kennedy and Sarah Morgan McKown as well as the post-war recollections of David Hunter Strother, Henry Kidd Douglas, Jedediah Hotchkiss, David H. Black, Belle Boyd, Susan Pitzer, Theodore Buser and others provide special insight into the events of the times.

Unpublished family histories, Bible notations and family oral tradition provide a unique body of information. Daisy Howard, descendant of James Myers, Pat Dellinger and Wallace L. Miller, descendants of Harvey Allen Miller, Harriet B. Wolf, descendent of Thadeus Britchner, Jane Snyder, descendent of Ambassador Charles James Faulkner, Craig L. Gay descendant of Caleb Simpson, Blanche M. Pitzer, descendant of W.R. Spiker, David Dailey, descendant of James H.C. Dailey,

Christopher Athey, descendant of Zedekiah W. Smith, Roland Markle descendent of John Markle, Pam Cresswell, descendant of William Rush Porterfield, Edythe Darrow and others have provided information that has vastly enriched my understanding of the Civil War in the Lower Shenandoah Valley.

OTHER BOOKS BY SUSAN CRITES:

The Lively Ghosts Series
Lively Ghosts of
The Eastern Panhandle of West Virginia

More Lively Ghosts
Union Ghosts
Confederate Ghosts
More Civil War Ghosts
Ghosts of Christmas Past
The Littlest Ghosts
Ghosts of Lost Loves

The Samantha Carter Mystery Series
Murder in Martinsburg
Murder at the Fair
Murder at Confederate Headquarters

Civil War in The Eastern Panhandle
The Children's Activity Book

The Civil War in the Eastern Panhandle
of West Virginia: A Book of Days

Popular Culture
Strange and Amusing Tales of
The Eastern Panhandle of West Virginia

*These books are available from the publisher
or wherever fine books are sold.*

ABOUT THE AUTHOR

Susan Crites is a well-respected authority on the Civil War in the lower Shenandoah Valley counties of Berkeley, Jefferson and Morgan. She is the popular author of numerous books about the area. Her Great-great-great-grandfather, James Robert Carter, served in the 22d Virginia Infantry from 1861 through the cessation of hostilities in 1865. Her proud Virginia family survived the Reconstruction Era but did not forget! She is a member of the John Quincy Adams Nadenbousch Chapter of the United Daughters of the Confederacy.